Printed by IngramSpark Books
Lightning Sources, Inc. P.O.
Box 503531
St. Louis, MO 64150-3531

Library of Congress Cataloging in-Publication Data

Colley, Albert S. Jr.

ISBN: 978-1-64440-064-7

Love is like the spirit: the energy never dies. Its influence is forever.

Dr. aLbert S. Colley, Jr.

AUTHOR'S COMMENTS

I read a book many years ago that I will not name, which changed my perspective on life leading me to stay in a flow and just let things happen and flow to me. After having believed in this premise over the years, comes these quotes that just flowed to me: walking, sleeping, sitting, traveling etc. It's amazing. This is the reason why I must share.

As a seeker of knowledge, I am more than pleased to share my original *Cross-generational, Inspiring, Awakening, Telling, Thought Provoking, Candid quotes/postings/perspectives with you, the reader. All postings will not be for everyone, nor are they intended to be.*

The content in this book is of an original nature by the author and is under copyright protection as to claim.

All original posts as known by me, the author, in this book are my truths and perspectives; and some may be controversial to some readers. However, no posts were meant to offend or written with intent of malice toward any individuals. They were written with the intent to invoke and evoke thinking and reaction on the readers' behalf. Some of these posts may be flagged.

The order of most of the quotes in this book were totally random and were written as they came to me.

1) It's not that someone can't make a decision that has not had the experience. It's just that someone who has had the experience is more intuitive in their decision.

2) To pluck a petal from a flower is akin to plucking a finger from a pianist. To totally pull it from the ground is even worse.

3) Life's a Journey: Remember you're your only competitor! Don't concern yourself with anyone else.

4) Now to matters at hand--
Crawl, walk, (one-step, two-step, three- step, four) skip, jump, run, fall, get-up; walk, skip, jump, run, fall, get-up; skip, jump, run, hurdle, (track mud) run, hurdle, stumble – fall? nope, run, run, run, Run. Destination GOAL!

5) A dream is only a dream if you can't remember it. Hey, if you remember the dream, then that wasn't a dream; that was REAL.

6) The soul/spirit does not belong to another man. The soul/spirit is the only true union between God and man. You come into this world with it, and it is the only thing you take with you when you leave this world. Every other personal part of you dies and is left behind.

7) A truce or promise thereof is a ruse, not to be trusted.

1) *To show humility is to mirror inner beauty, strength, and power.*

2) Art can imitate Life; but Art can't trump Life.

3) There is no reality, only one's perception of the moment.

4) If you only had but one dime, you could tighten several screws,

5) Here comes life   -   Catch It.

6) A Black male's journey is nothing, but a series of steps usually guided by the matriarch of the family. Baby steps, umbrella steps for a rainy day; and giant steps to achieve your dreams. In memory of John Coltrane

Dear Deer in the Headlights,

1) Racism is a disease, and a cure has yet to be found. It is like Aids: It mutates, morphs, and evolves albeit slow and steady. Then it reaches a crescendo until it

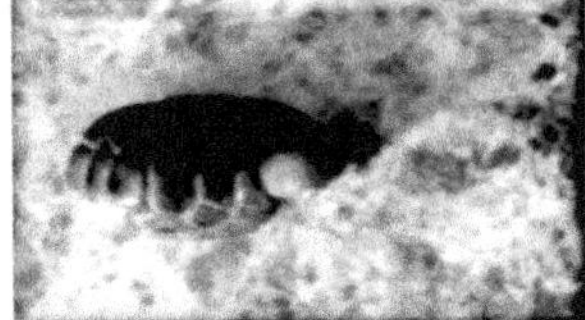

eventually explodes.

2) Figure out who you are and what you're about first., and then some things will begin to fall into place.

3) Stand up either for it or against it but stand up.

4) Dreaming is like praying: You can do it anywhere; You can do it anytime; You can do it alone; It's personal and it's more of things to come.

5) Start asking kids, "What is your dream?"

Photographer ASCjr

1) A wise man knows what he doesn't know and enters discussion accordingly.

2) In a mad world, the only way to be safe is to be mad.

3) Prejudice can be attributed partially to heredity as cancer or diabetes. It doesn't mean you're going to be stricken with it, but you sure are predisposed.

Dear Deer in the Headlights,

4) I've forgotten more than I remember.

1) Final say on the comma: When in doubt, Don't (You'll be right more times than wrong.)

2) Sometimes the ones who were supposed to love you the most are sometimes the ones who try the hardest to keep you from being who you are.

3) The question is: How long can we withstand humanness?

4) Lawmakers of states, governments, and municipalities have no jurisdiction over the laws of the Universe.

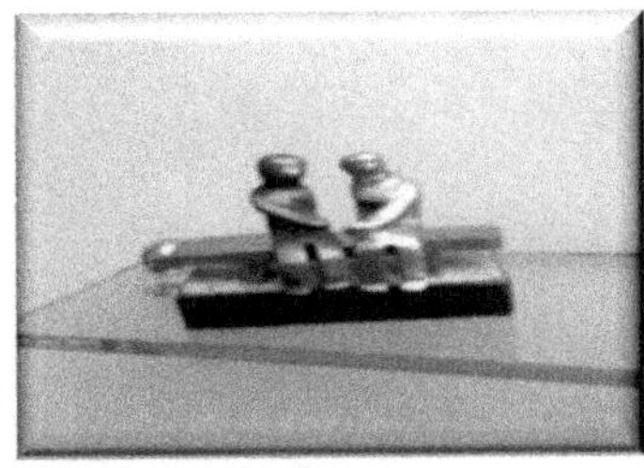

5) You can't legislate feelings.

1) "Bromance" The love between two males without sexual attraction or involvement; the step between platonic and the sexual aspect of a male-on-male relationship; akin to the feeling between/among teammates after winning a top sport's game.

2) Not to take a risk is the only risk not to take.

3) Look for tomorrow; yesterday was a glance.

4) It's not what you have; it's when you use it.

Rene Magritte 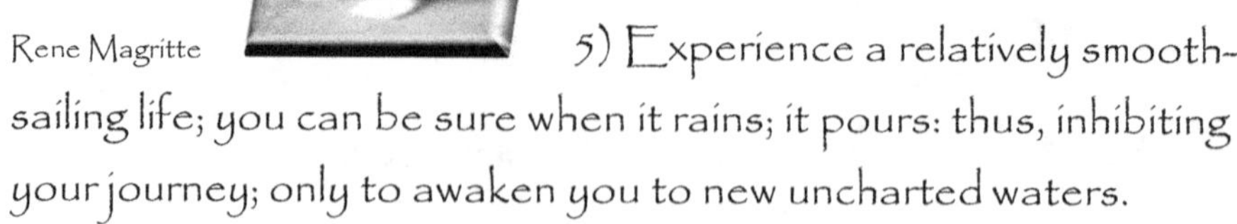 5) Experience a relatively smooth-sailing life; you can be sure when it rains; it pours: thus, inhibiting your journey; only to awaken you to new uncharted waters.

1) Marriage is you being you and me being me in the presence of each (an)other.

2) See me through the Day anyway you wanna; Give it to me anyway you wanna; Take it any way you wanna; Be whomever you wanna, wanna be when we're together; Cuff me and jail me if you wanna. Keep me informed if you wanna; Let's live life together if you wanna. Say a prayer for me if you wanna.

3) A true leader is not interested in dividing for the benefit of a few but unifying for the benefit of all.

4) Racism ---- Is there a cure on the horizon?

5) Time is relative, No?

6) It takes discipline to be disciplined in a discipline.

1) *Mature read only* - Sometimes gayness gets too hung-up on the sexual technique and theory of the gay existence that gay people tend to shun and obliterate their own humanity. It is not always important to go for a "love fest", a dark (k)night, a "thug" love, a "meet me in St. Louie (baseball)" to have a validated existence.

2) Don't spend a lot of time pursuing goals not in alignment with your purpose in life.

3) Every person has a purpose for being here. Finding and knowing what that purpose "IS" as elusive as discovering the true meaning of "Life."

4) Don't be affected by the mundane musings of life.

1) Some bridges are meant to be dismantled, once used.

2) Perceptions can change as positions get further away, (mirrors surrounding you).

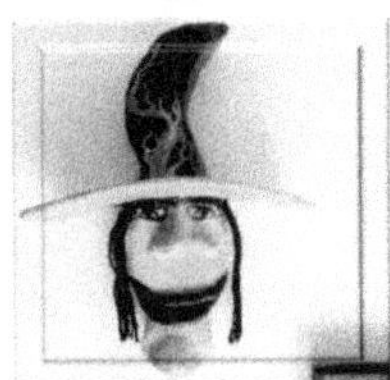

Photo ASCjr

3) Self-doubt is the bulldozer of dreams.

4) Power is as natural to human existence as air, so why misuse it?

Dear Deer in the Headlights

5) Yesterday is forever; tomorrow might be.

6) Don't ever doubt your decisions; for doubt is the precursor to defeat.

1) Life is like running down a football field: You hope you find a hole and hope you don't get tackled as you go for the goal.

2) When you've climbed to the mountaintop once, don't be goaded into trying to prove it again; for that peak has already been reached.

3) You are the microcosm of the Universe - a Universe of microcosm(s).

4) Anything natural is better than something artificial.

Photo ASCjr

5) It's not about being adversarial; it's about being proverbial.

1) It can never get to "there," unless there is first a "here."

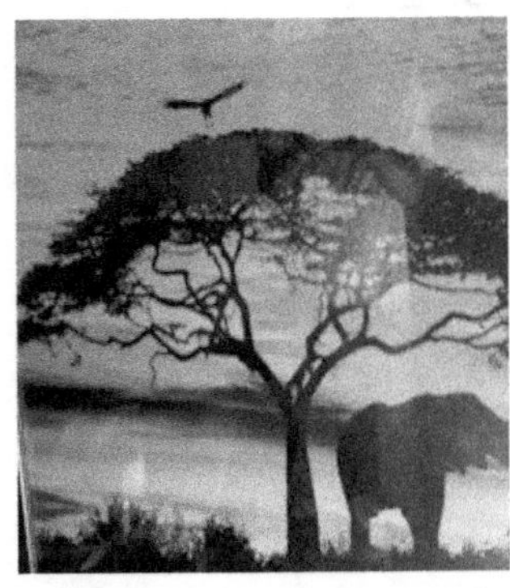

2) Our DNA is made of the same DNA as a tree: when we exhale, the tree breathes; when the tree exhales, we breathe.

3) Now that you're totally clear on your side of the issue, how about the other side?

4) Those who are closed to learning are doomed to be a slave to ignorance.

5) (Surmise) Unfortunately, generally speaking, in many instances in the United States, the criminal justice system and on our city streets, a man of color is presumed guilty (starting at 0 and working his way to 100) until proven innocent vs. a white man, being presumed innocent (starting at 100 and working his way to 0) until proven guilty. (Just sayin')

1) Sad. But, one's color and one's approximation to whiteness is devalued or valued around the globe.

2) Can you make me a poem  made-up/out of snowflakes? 

3) You know why I love life because I love all the life-

forms that surround me.   photo ASCjr

4) Luck is where opportunity meets possibility.

5) Remember you did it out of love, and what you do out of love cannot be wrong.

6) Racism is one of the founding bedrocks of America – took root in a rock (Plymouth Rock). You can strike it, only blood and weariness will flow.

Navy Pier

Photo ASCjr

1) Is there any one combination of musical notes that's not taken? rhythms, arpeggios? Then that only leaves accents and tones.

Wall Street Journal Picture of the week 5/31/14

2) If you had to be clean or hungry, be clean.

3) The breath is the zero in Life.

1)   If you had only the choices of ride or walk; walk.

2) Do not doubt your experiences and the lessons they taught you.

3) If you want to know what to do after 50, take a hint from the eagle and jellyfish.

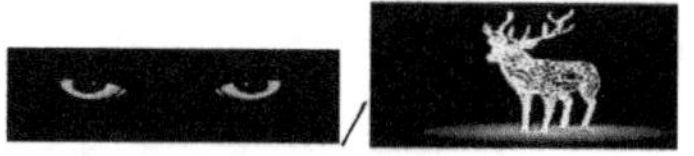

4) White privilege is undeserved: the only requirement is being born white; black privilege is non-existent.

5) Happiness is like the horizon: always there, but never fully reached.

6) In your sixties you should understand what your purpose for being is.

7) The concept of "before" has no meaning without the concept of time.

1)   Whenever you think about saying, 'I wish..., instead say, "I think I would love it if...

2) *II ππ* Everything in moderation: Eat on the <u>fly,</u> just a little; be careful if you get <u>high,</u> just a little; think with the 3rd <u>eye(ey),</u> just a little; say <u>hi</u> when arriving and <u>bye</u> when leaving, but sometimes – just a little; ok to be <u>bi,</u> just a little; men bow and neck <u>tie,</u> just a little; be a good <u>guy</u>/ bad guy, just a little; <u>sigh,</u> just a little; <u>cry,</u> just a little; be <u>shy,</u> just a little; if you must, tattoo the <u>thigh,</u> just a little; hey, hey, hey - just a little; nay, nay, nay - just a little; reach to the <u>sky,</u> just a little; <u>dive,</u> just a little; DIE, just a little. (now read the rhyming underlined words rhythmically, just a little.)

3) The clothes don't make the man; the man who wears the clothes "the" clothes make.

4) Be honest and genuine.

5) Stop saying "Yeah, if" And just compliment a brother.

6) Imagine this world without you.

1) *A baby girl's unspoken message to her father:*
As I awake from the protection of your loving arms-still amazed by my new presence; pick me up. I cry a cry of happiness, then smile and clutch you with my little fingers to let you know "I love you, daddy."

2) It takes discipline to be disciplined in a discipline.

3) Be who you are and say what you feel because those who mind, don't matter; and those who matter, don't mind.

Dear Deer in the Headlights,

4) Cherish what you have, and you'll love what else comes your way.

5) Roll with the tide or roll over the tide. Never let the tide take you under.

6) If you are black in the court system, "justice can be blind" to your humanity.

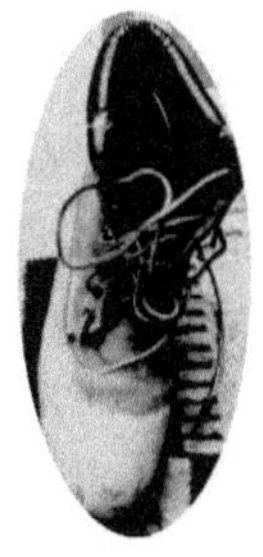

1) Some say animals are becoming more like humans. If animals are becoming more like humans; then are humans becoming more something else (or) are the animals just catching up.? (Just Sayin')

2) Innocence cannot be granted, replaced, rebuilt (such as self-esteem) substituted, retrieved, nor borrowed; sadly, it sometimes encounters the worst taken or put up for sale.

3) *Caring people, nurture people.*

4) *Know what you know, but you will get your boost from knowing what you don't know.*

5) *When you find out who you are, you will realize why you're here.*

6) *Don't think about all the reasons something can't work and focus on the one reason why it will work.*

1) Anything natural has more credibility than something artificial.

2) We are driven by 3-things: the experiences we have; the experiences we think we want to have; and the experiences we decide we want.

3) As an educator, I don't see color or size; only skill, talent, and heart. What I look forward to is that light bulb inside of you to light.

4) Fasting is voluntary; hunger is relative; starvation is forced and rear and could be the last stop in this train we call life.

5) If you had only two choices: ride or walk; walk.

6) Do not doubt your experiences, and the lessons they taught you.

7) Everyone is born a genius; the <u>process of life</u> "de 'genius' tizes" one.

1) Nature never breaks her own laws.

2) There is no wiser move than to seize and take ownership of a "moment" in time.

3) Treachery is the wine of cowards.

4) Take flight; now level off.

Deer in the Headlights,
5) Is there anything more to life than a breath?

6) To deny the spirit is to deny one's existence; for this is what makes you the unique person you are.

7) No regrets: Never let anything or anyone override your passion for your passion.

1) Especially, have concern and even compassion sometimes for those who have not been as blessed as you.

2) Live life in the lane that is comfortable for you, even though others might pass you by and others lag.

Dear Deer in the Headlights, 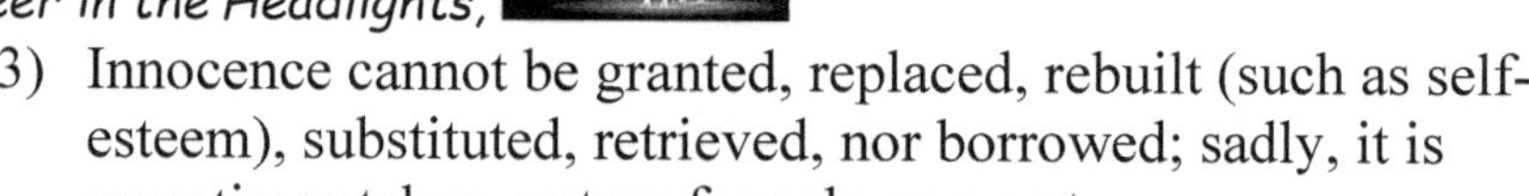

3) Innocence cannot be granted, replaced, rebuilt (such as self-esteem), substituted, retrieved, nor borrowed; sadly, it is sometimes taken, put up for sale or worst.

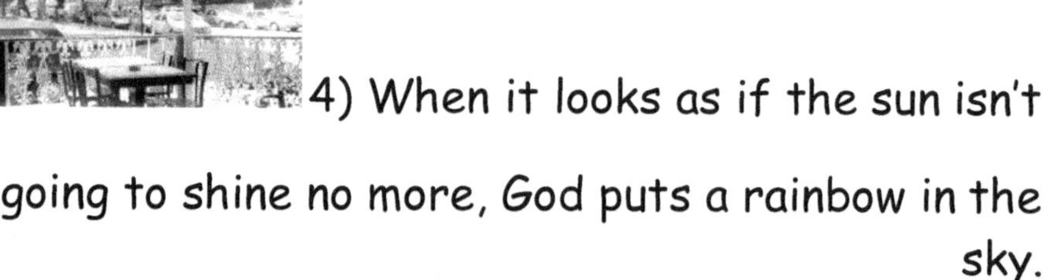

4) When it looks as if the sun isn't going to shine no more, God puts a rainbow in the sky.

5) There are universal tenets that operate on both sides of the railroad tracks.

1) What we think, we speak; what we speak, we write; what we write, we read.

2) Let that baby (girl) be born.  

3) My only regret when I die: I have not done all I wanted or needed to do in this earthly realm.

4) Preparation, Application, Implementation.

5) **Perceived end–of–Life is like a caterpillar's doomed perception; only to become this triumphant butterfly. So, fret not, the scourge of death it is but, a temporary fleeting reality.**

6) **Many times, people who are diagnosed with Alzheimer's disease don't wander off, but run away like a misunderstood teenager; thus, once an adult; twice a child.**

1) If you listen to an older person, you will know what's around that corner before you turn it.

2) In an unknown city, immediately get a point of reference.

3) There are two ways to learn life's hard lessons: a) someone telling you, and you 'listen'; or b) you run into a "brick wall" and everything in your fiber tells you this is real, forcing you to listen. ASCSr.

4) Older people are not slower in thinking or remembering; they have more in their heads than most young people; therefore, prompting slower processing and response.

Dear Deer in the Headlights ,

5) What's a day without the sun; what's a night without a moon; what's a life without the one you love?

6) Lack is the "bomb" we impose on ourselves.

1) *If you must leave, leave softly and with the least disruption; although disruption there will be.*

2) *Hate is lethal to the one who harbors it.*

3) *If the world were square,*  *you could corner the enemy.*

4) { 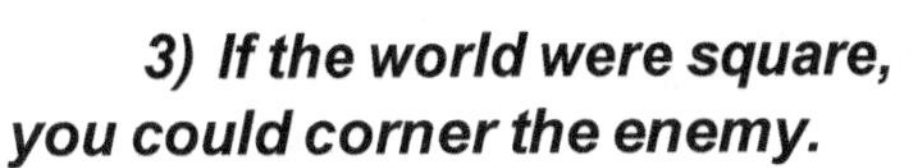 Schwab} because if you do, your tomorrow and tomorrows will be better.

5) *Making someone laugh is the first step to a friendship/relationship.*

6) *Inspired, I am; Enthused, I'm not.*

7) *Hold on to your better hand; that's why you have two.*

8) A thing of unquestionable beauty takes its own picture.

1) If you had to regret anything about your life when that "hour" comes, regret you didn't get to do and/or have achieved everything you wanted to achieve.

 **2) As you live; you breathe.**

http://Vimeo.com/55644502

3) It is so. (Amen).

4) But I swear-if I had to get back in the game, you would regret it.

**5) Embrace and release your inner 'bē- - ătch'
(however you define that).**

*6) Sometimes life – like numbers - is/are an enigma:
14=1+4(5), 5+2=7, 7+16=23, 23+14=37+4=41. Now,*

*14+7+23+37+41=122+1= 1 2 3.
0 divided by 0 (Hmm.)*

1) Never underestimate a man; always overestimate him that way you increase your chances of winning.

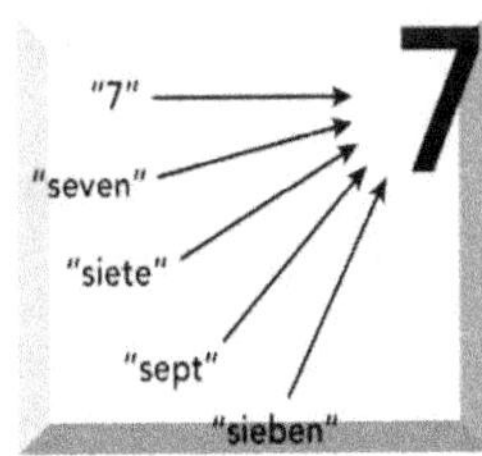

2) If you want to make "heads or tails tell tales" of where you're going, connect the dots of where you've been.

3) Praying is like dreaming: You can do it anywhere; you can do it at any time; you can do it alone; it's personal; and it's a hope of things to come.

4) Perceived end-of-life is like a caterpillar's perception only to become this magnificent butterfly. So, fret not - the scourge of death is but fleeting only to metamorphosize into a beautiful state of being.

1) Am I but a butterfly fleeing into the arms of time to embrace the secret and beauty I alone possess?

2) Are you but a dream only to surface as a reality when needed?
(think about it)

3) The first word you should know in a foreign language if you're traveling abroad is how to say the word 'help' in the native language.

4) Perceptions, perspectives, and interpretations tell the story: Perceptions are dictated by one's experiences at present and in the past; perspectives are dictated by one's vantage point. Interpretations are dictated by other's experiences.

5) In heaven, there is no currency other than self.

1) An eye for an eye leaves the whole world blind.

2) You should never have to apologize for being who you are.

3) *Sometimes what you know can get in the way of what you need to know.*

4) *Don't be a Whackadoodle*

5) *Breathing is but my breath, airing a concern.*

6) Greet the sunrise/sunset, lake. Oh, shimmering, rippling lake. *https://www.youtube.com/watch?v=ZemvBdRLg4k*

7) *"I had no choice." You always have a choice. You just happen to make the wrong one.*

1) Space is the chasm we exist in without our awareness of being there; thus, miraculously become no place is really an actual place.

2) White is a condition, not a color.

Dear Deer in the Headlights,

3) A thing of unquestionable beauty takes its own picture.

4) The English language provides you with the abundance of words to not almost express what you mean, but to express exactly what you mean.

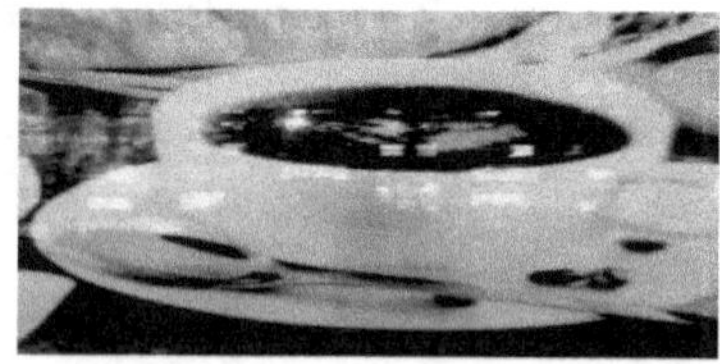

5) Start off right and it'll end up right.

1) I don't know if I'll be alive tomorrow; but I know I had a hellavu time today.

2) It's one thing to live life to its fullest; it's another thing to live life recklessly.

3) Once you look at the big picture, look at the whole picture before commenting.

4) What do I know for sure: That I will fulfill my destiny despite myself.

5) Additionally, it's about being able to totally confide in someone; it's about not having to testify in a court of law about your spouse; not being banned from seeing someone in a hospital because you are not a relative; who decides if you'll live or die; and things that are only available to married couples.

1) When we die, the consciousness of our existence as we experienced in life becomes non-existent; and from all reasonable perspectives, never existed: This is not saying that we did exist. You see, the physical body in death I still see; the consciousness that went along with that physical body
- gone, non-existent.

2) I only try to know what I don't know.

3) On cooking - It's not the 'how much'; it's the 'what'.

4) Clarification is in order and should always be given an opportunity to express itself because more times than not it proves to be useful in coming/arriving at a decision/conclusion.

5) Every sensation intensifies with age; the worst being pain.

6) Do you have a tenuous relationship with the truth?

7) You feel better when you accomplish something new rather than when you receive something new.

HIKE

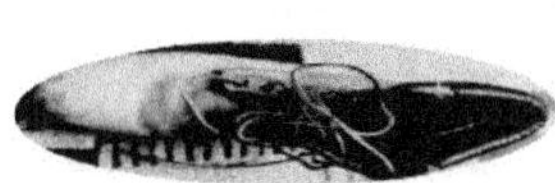

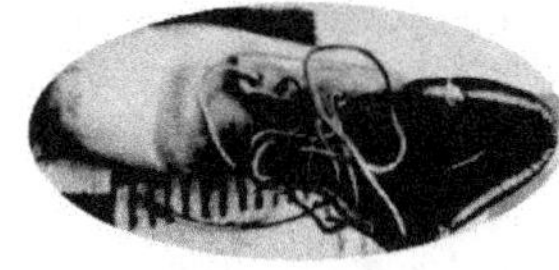

HIKE

NEW YORK "Manhattan" NEXUS

(an Ode) **Circa 1979**

Observed and Written by

copyrighted 1984/**revised 2014**

https://www.dropbox.com/home?preview=New+York+Nexus+Colley.m4a

(Author's piano rendering)

Ellis Island

https://www.youtube.com/watch?v=x7CIgWZTdgw

The New York Yankees

Babe Ruth "The Bambino", Joe DiMaggio, Mickey Mantle, Ty Cobb, Elston Howard, A-Rod, Whitey Ford, Jerry Jeter, Yogi Berra, Casey Stengel, Reggie Jackson, Lou Gehrig, and others

The New York Jets, Knicks, Mets, Brooklyn Nets, Globetrotters, *And*

THE BROADWAY MUSICAL POST WORLD WAR II

West Side Story, Sound of Music, Rent, Hair, My Fair Lady, Pippin', Applause, Cabaret, Carousel,
The King and I, Flower Drum Song, Godspell, 42nd Street, Oliver, The Music Man, Legally Blond,
Guys and Dolls, Chicago, Bye, Bye Birdie, Peter Pan, Wicked, No Strings, Evita, Shrek, State Fair, Cher,
Damn Yankees, Gypsy, Aladdin, Ragtime, Funny Girl, Hello Dolly, Golden Boy, Camelot, Jumbo, Motown,
Avenue Q, Pajama Game, The Book of Mormon, Phantom of the Opera, Hamilton, Company, Tootsie, Cats,
The Last Ship, Lion King, Kinky Boots, Sweet Charity, Hairspray, Xanadu, South Pacific, Annie, Pal Joey,
Les Misérables, Billy Elliot, Miss Saigon, Beautiful, Jesus Christ Superstar, Jersey Boys, The Visit, Frozen,
Fiddler on the Roof, Carnival, Sister Act, Sweeny Todd, In the Heights, Dreamgirls, Newsies, Footloose,
The Fantasticks, Million Dollar Quartet, The Producers, Smoky Joe's Café, Mama Mia, Purlie, Waitress,
Paint Your Wagon, Fun House, Matilda, Stop the World – I Want to Get Off, Promises, Promises, Grease,
Come From Away, Finian's Rainbow, La Cage aux Folles, Bullets Over Broadway, Can-Can, Summer,
The Wiz, St. Louis Woman, School of Rock, SpongeBob Square Pants, Bruce Springsteen on Broadway,
'Ain't Misbehavin', An American in Paris, Roar of the Greasepaint "The Smell of the Crowd," Candide,
Anything Goes, How to Succeed in Business Without Really Trying, Silk Stockings, Pretty Woman,
Sweet Charity, Tina, Ain't to Proud to Beg, You're a Good Man Charlie Brown, Mame,
Dear Evan Hansen, Arms too Short to Box with God, and others

Overture

New York, New York:
microcosm of the world,
enthralling city; city of many live- (life)times.

Manhattan:
Hudson River, East River
Greenwich Village, Harlem,
Central Park.

I have seen
people prevail
In~ luxury~ on Sutton Place;

A woman erect
a shelter from cardboard boxes
on a Madison Avenue doorstep.

hustlers advance

Terrence Howard

and
linger for the next
curiosity seeker.

First Movement

*See
lovers take*

carriage rides.

*Hear
people articulate
many different tongues
in the streets.*

See 

*the streetlights explode
and the marquises
awake as curtain time
draws near.*

*See
People
in Greenwich Village
chess-checking
on life.*

Listen...Shh

4

Feel
the pulse of
Rockefeller Center
Glistening ice
in the frigid air
ice skaters of all ages

and
nationalities
swirling,

whirling
to music of the same
drummer.

See
Central Park
by
day and night
reflect

on Walden Pond.

Second Movement

Move to the
Subway system
with its
up/
down tunnels—
BMT, IRT: 8th, 6th Avenue

Life Magazine 1944

Line Passengers different as the world
this city represent(s).

See
the clothiers,
food vendors,
diamond merchants
peddle their wares
on the street
and
in their districts.

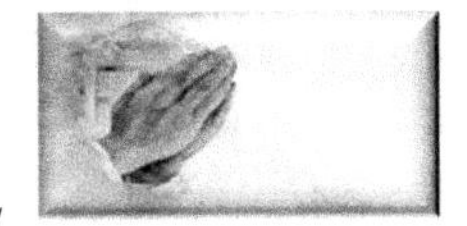

Pray

men preach

the Word

of God from

campers

along the most infamous

stretch of Broadway.

> *Stay*
> *rock musicians*
> *proclaim the word*
> *of Jesus and*
> *tell of the last days*
> *through music and verse.*

See and hear

the jazzman,

classical

and

country-western

play

along the by-way

in Greenwich Village

> *and*

on Broadway

for a handful of onlookers

To stop; to listen; and, perhaps
> *Drop*
an offering in their

open

instrument case.

Third Movement

*Seen
restaurants flourish;
beggars stand
in the mission line.*

*Seen

Blacks*

Bill "Bojangles" Robinson www.*youtube*.com/watch?v=AjCFYpWDmfM

*black-tap back
over a century-worn
bridge.*

Seen ◯ ◯
*Bowery Boys
rally
for a
life loss.*

*Seen
fortune tellers
beckon
fortune seekers
from
open windows
and
open doorways.*

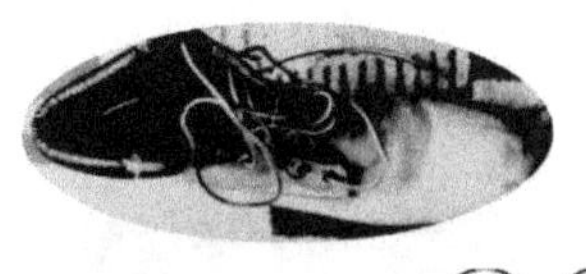

Seen

dreamers

lead/

pigeons

feed

emotional disease in the square

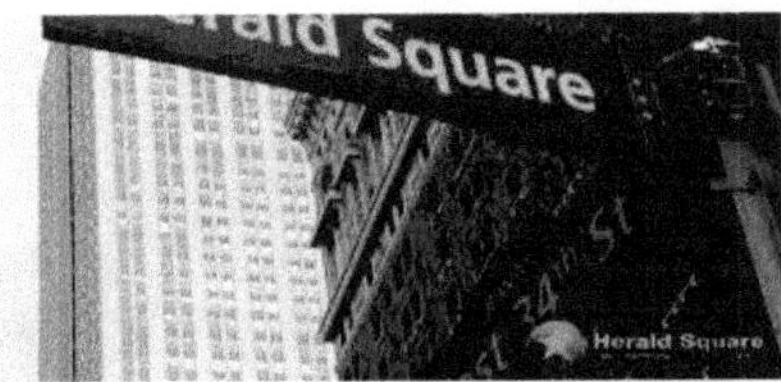

on 34th (Herald Square) and Broadway

Jam traffic.

Won't be long.

Roll

Taxis:

Grand Central baggage please.

LaGuardia – Flight 151

Port Authority

Leaving in 20-minutes

JFK.

Hang

night people.

Trash collectors

let you know.

Saunter

Sneaker

children.

Connect---
Gay lovers. Hold Hands.

Work Wall Street

Ella Fitzgerald   Billie Holiday   Tony Bennett   Frank Sinatra

*Sing, **Song** **S**ingers*

https://www.youtube.com/watch?v=2r9Yhw3n1LY

Fred Astaire

Gregory Hines

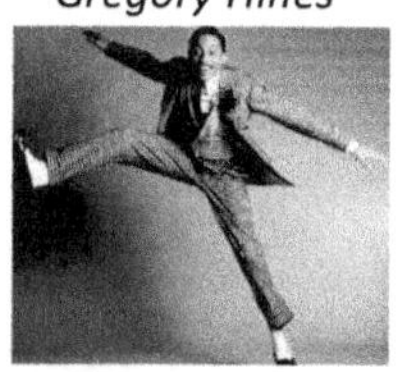

Dance, <u>dance</u> dancers.

https://www.youtube.com/watch?v=mAB12ael6nA
https://www.youtube.com/watch?v=nlpvhtd1ual

Act Actors! Act!

Dam\it~ ~~Release fire hydrant in the summer~ ~ Heat.

Fourth Movement

Think  *about*
a refugee
plays
the music
his homeland
forbids him
to (x) press.

The pinball wizard

plunk
his ivory
as melodic notes
ring
through Central Park.

Throngs
of people.

A young man
parade
a sandwich board,
"I need a JOB."

11
Learned men
exists
on subway platforms.
Hunger and despair
in their eyes.
(hungry for the man they were;
despair over the man they've become.

A Man
on the Avenue
polish the soles of

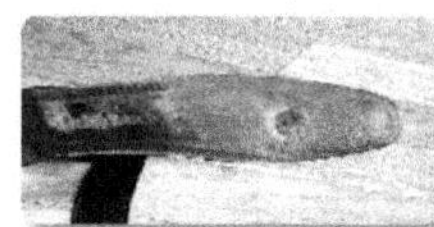

his shoes
in an attempt
to hide
the weariness
of his eternal soul.

A stand-up
comic perform
in Washington Square
to a capacity crowd.
Laughter!
The pass
of a worn hat.
What is his name?
Do New Yorkers have names?

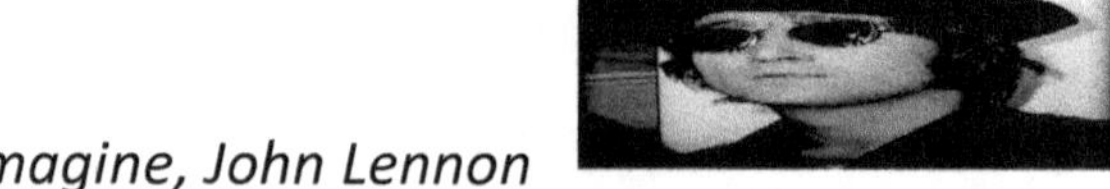

Imagine, John Lennon
murdered
and
eulogized
72nd Central Park West;
Let It Be.

https://www.youtube.com/watch?v=aWfQ04FuaVY

Fifth Movement

SEE ◯ ◯
New York
Museum of Metropolitan Art.

New York, New York

New York's
Old
Coney Island.

New York
Zoo;
New York
Ellis Island
and

gaze

out at the Atlantic Ocean

where many

have crossed

jus to say

"America, my home."

An African American
A-man called
"nigger"
in the (rock me in the) 'bosom'

DON'T BLINK

of Lincoln Centre/

Heed
helmeted
helmsmen
at the helm
(in the name of law and order)
man
the streets
of Harlem
ready to do battle
at the first sign.

Damn Yankees

Photo ASCjr

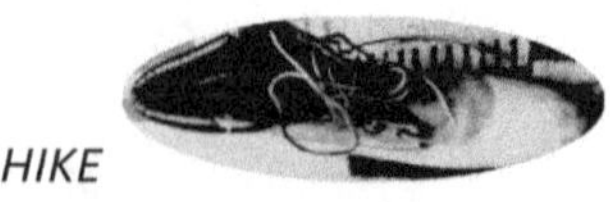

HIKE

14

Sixth Movement

Observe

Greeks

Operate

delicatessens and shoe shops;

and

Chipmunks dine

in the park.

Iranians

Operate

a paper stand:

and

Me and the

caged Polar Bear

pace

out of

our natural habitat.

Chinese
Operate
laundries;
and
fortune
does not
smile.
Japanese

operate
cleaners;
and
teenagers
pay homage
to their electronic
gods.

Puerto Ricans
own
operate
barber shops and fruit stands;
and
dealers drug tourists.
East Indians
operate
a hotel;
and
Roaches
commit
suicide. (Really?)

Italians
own
chemical companies;
and fairy tales
cease.

Blacks

operate

run

secretarial services and churches

and

the legacy lives on.

Anglo-Saxons

Owning,

operating,

running

restaurants, insurance agencies, employment agencies,

bookstores, movie houses, banks

and Christians

pray

at St. Patrick's Cathedral.

However,
me, microcosm
man
puzzle
as paradoxical
irony
marches
on.

Seventh Movement (Epilogue)

The same heeded
helmeted helmsman
line
Broadway
From
Times Square
To 45th

In 

limousines and carriages

Make
their way
through
part avenues and streets
to Sardi's and the like;
oblivious
to the masses...
(Something's Happening Mid-town)

10th 9$^{t\,h}$ 8$^{t\,h}$ 7th 6th 5th 4th 3rd 2nd 1st
https://www.youtube.com/watch?v=rgusCINe260

It's all smoke and mirrors

CLOUDGATE

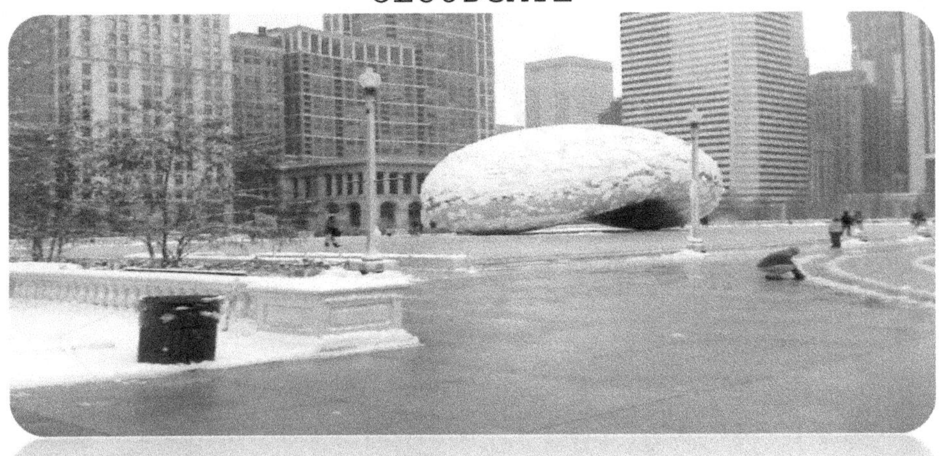

aka "The Bean" Millennium Park, Chicago
Photo by ASCjr

CHI

Chicago, double barrel city
Double-edge hunter of the coasts
Fulcrum of the nation

Rough-dried at the sleeves and
Collar-pressed in the middle by
The iron politics that rule.
ASCjr

Bottled Chicago Wind at Dawn (listen)
https://www.dropbox.com/s/66a5cnv3puzpmzg/Bottled%20Chicagp%20Wind%20-%20God.m4a?dl=0

Photo ASCjr

1) I didn't care about how much he has or where he lived, only that he was a friend of mine.

2) In the physical realm, matter cannot be destroyed; therefore, our physical bodies are not destroyed when we die but recycled in the Universe for only the Creator knows What.

3) Babies come from the union of two "Souls," making one soul. This is one reason why blood on both sides of family will be family in perpetuity.

4) Death is only a lull in life until our next assignment.

5) Death is inevitable; life is not.

- Bloomin' rHigHt....

  - How deep is the ocean (which one?); How high (high) is the sky (high?) Song Lyric, (Answer this question from a beginning and posit a reasonable conclusion, and I'd say you are ready to move on. Where that be? Well. Your call. () http://www.youtube.com/watch?v=xU2RICOKynw&sns=em

- Being courteous and kind is nothing more than humanity at work.

  - We believe what we perceive; we perceive what we believe.

- Live your life and forget age.

- Success is never having to explain yourself, of course, unless you want to.

Dear Deer in the Headlights,

- # The wind is the soul's vehicle.

- **The Spirit is the wind.: It carries/moves souls from place to place on the earth and beyond to ensure the souls' continued existence.**

Sounds of Pure Recorded Wind

https://www.dropbox.com/s/yt5xlyklsokz9dw/mp3Early%20%20Morning%20Wind.mp3?dl=0

Have you ever thought about what ' ' is a miracle?
(Just Sayin')

- Have you ever thought about what is the color of a miracle?

<u>IT MIGHT STAY HOT FOREVER</u> (lyric and music by author)

My heart longs to be free; My heart told me so.

I long for the good life; no strife-and carefree.
The nights nev-er ended; the days had got lone-ly
My heart had to learn to breathe a-gain.
I walk in the nightclub; my new baby's there.
I'm shown to the table
I start to feel the air.
She leans o-ver to kiss me…
This has got to be the life.
I feel carefree and no strife.

IT MIGHT STAY HOT FORVER

The groo-vi-est set is about to be-gin,
The la-dies are sway-ing
Cause JAZZ is still in.

The sax-o-phone play-er sounds
Just like a Coltrane.

The trum-pet play-er blows some
Cool, way-out Jazz.
The set is the mel-low-ist yet!

The band ends the set with
Miles' "So What."

The au-di-ence wants the guys
To play a-no-ther Cut
The bar-ten-der yells,
"Last Call for Alcohol"
The set winds down once a-gain.

WE walk out the door,
The taxis right there.
My ba-by and I
Be-gin to feel the air.
Our hearts are to-ga-ther;

Our mind becomes one.   *The end of the sto-ry has just be-gun.*

IT MIGHT STAY HOT FOREVER

https://www.dropbox.com/s/ulbt0ybcmbfe9xl/It%20Might%20Stay%20Hot%20Forever.m4a?dl=0

(if you can't be with the wine you Love,)

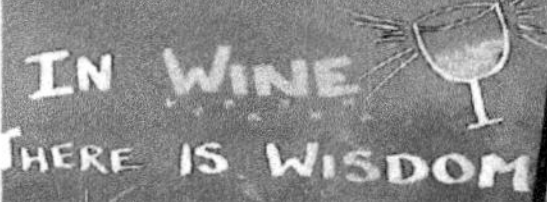

Manhattan on therocks

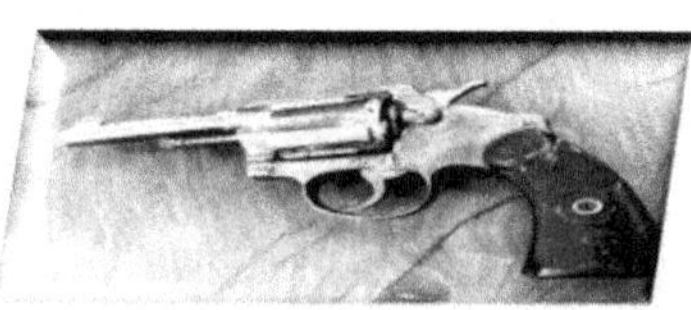

The "revolver"

2-parts bourbon; 1-part Patron XO Café or Mr. Black liquer

1-Drop of orange or peach bitters

Shake it in a shaker with ice; Pour it into a martini glass

Optional: a strawberry or 4-blueberries or b

NO MORE POWDER BLUES (lyric and music by author)

My life wants to breathe a-gain.

I fin-al-ly got home.

My days are long...nights are free...soul is on its own.

The Sun is bright.

Moon is high...

My Life is fresh a-gain.

I'm out front...I just now can love a-gain.

NO MORE POWDER BLUES FOR ME

I'm up to be all of me.

NO MORE POWER BLUES FOR ME

I'm up to be all I can be.

My heart wants to fly a-way.

Can't seem to slow down.

My mind is set.

You can bet.

Feet on solid ground.

I have sur-vive-d

All the pain

Of a Love gone bad.

NO MORE POWDER BLUES FOR ME.

I'm born to Be all I can Be.

NO MORE POWDER BLUES FOR ME

https://youtu.be/YIJG8_DU5wg

https://www.dropbox.com/s/gnd6g09353i99uu/No%20More%20Powderwith%20acoustic%20drumbeatm4a.m4a?dl=0

https://www.dropbox.com/s/lywbqiyqzd71mht/No%20More%20Powder%20Blues%20Music.m4a?dl=0

37

(The following statement is to inform, not to incite) To understand the anger of a people you must first understand the centuries of pain that caused that anger: DARKNESS — INTOMORNIN Hunted; trapped; dis-respected; beaten; dehumanized (labeled as property); victimized; sold; bartered; bred like cattle; subjugated; maimed; raped (women, men, and children); lynched; bastardized; separated; degraded; menaced; terrorized; humiliated; hated and stripped of any and all dignity, ETC., by whom? America's Caucasian forefathers.

And then blacks hear from a people whose ancestry was guilty of all these horrendous acts the insulting/hurting statement (usually delivered in a very matter of fact tone and way): GET OVER IT," as if this was nothing more than a guy standing up a girl for a date. Well, I'm here to tell you that with that statement; blacks relive the horrors of white, not black, disgrace all over again. Blacks don't need condescension; they need comforting and understanding of what their people endured.

No other people in the world who have been subject by even a portion of the indignities blacks had to face are told to "Get Over It." Case in point: "You can't turn a corner in Warsaw that you don't see some memorial, some evidence of World War II and the Holocaust." Ronald Balsan   "

The ravishes and consequences of slavery are so deep that even today there is no way to measure it, explain it, rationally deal with it, deny it, and did I add, certainty not gotten over. Most people can't get over gaining weight and you want a whole race of people (not 3/5 of one) to get over the tens of thousands who were mistreated that an entire system condone for centuries during slavery. Well, think again! Yes, "Black Lives Matter," however, here we are in 2016 still trying to convince the power structure of this.

Reality: Whites fear of Blacks is rooted in white guilt.

War on Drugs. Stop and Frisk. All Lives Matter (a diversion). Make America Great Again. And of course, the granddaddy of them all posited by one of the most corrupt presidents (Richard Nixon) in American History, Law and Order, which was the one that started the mass incarceration in this country of minorities: all winks of the eye for those bigots it was intended. Come on, guys, minorities are much smarter than that!

Man-up, see it for what it was and the reality of what it still is, and sincerely convince black people you care and understand their anger and will assist in any way you can to make the wounds of the horrendous institution of slavery today and yesterday burn a little less. Is that too much to ask? And if you can' bring yourself to do that at least don't ever say to a black person, "Get over it."

So now, let's all step back and take heed from those lyrics in Michael Jackson's "Man in the Mirror.": 'I'm starting with the man in the mirror. So, if you wanna make a better place, just look at yourself and then *MAKE THAT CHANGE.* https://youtu.be/ljp/OneGk2Q

<u>*Ed.D. on Effective Leadership*</u>

1) Leadership is relative to the leader and the audience being served by that leader/leadership.

2) As the needs of the audience change so must the style and direction of the leader/leadership change.

3) Conversely, the audience the leadership serves must understand the need for flexibility.

4) Leadership is neither literal nor static but a living, breathing entities. It is within these breathing organizations come to life. Without this breath, an organization dies.

5) The organization is the entire organism, which must maintain the heart; for without this heart the organization also dies.

6) Good leaders have lifelines and know when to use them: In or outside of the organization whose opinion you respect and trust and whom you respect and trust personally.

a) Family member whom you have trust. B) Know the focal person in your organization/each department, even maintenance. Use these people as resources and sometimes the basis for and making decisions.

C) Organization/ departmental consensus. This can be department heads or simply rank and file.

> *Aside: to test an employee's loyalty don't hesitate to use the "cut the baby in half".*

If you just don't have a lifeline, you need to rely on:

a) What do the experts say on any given subject?

b) Weigh the pluses and minuses of a decision. Note: You can use a lifeline's advice as one of the minuses.

c) Don't underestimate going with your GUT.

d) Don't underestimate "sleeping on it."

e) Don't make a decision when tired.

f) Learn from a past mistake; don't make it twice.

1) **The) Soul is like God, you can't touch it, but it can touch you: and it does.**

2) **Soul is like the most perfect shape in the universe, the circle: It has no beginning and no end. Thus, like God, the Soul just "IS"; and therefore, by its very nature cannot be <u>completely</u> defined or comprehended.**

3) **Feeling, hearing, seeing, tasting, and smelling is a big part of the Soul. Once you physically die, those senses leave you but remain somewhere just as your wit, love, compassion, etc.**

4) God is all that's seen and unseen; imagined and yet unimagined and to be imagined.

5) God was the Internet before the Internet.

<u>GOD – MY ALL</u> (lyric and music by author)

God
Is
So
Good
To
Me.
He is my Light
When dark-ness comes.

And
God
Is
So
Right
For
Me.
He keeps
My hopes alive.
HE IS MY FRIEND.

(refrain)
God Knows all
Of my needs.
He knows all
Of my dreams.
He knows
Eve-ry-thing
On earth
And in heav-en a-bove.

(refrain II)
And God is my Light;
And God is my Might;
He is my Strength;
He is my Life;
He is the Way.

Yes, God is my ALL...

https://www.dropbox.com/s/hdnk9s04rdjobhe/God%20Is%20my%20All.m4a?dl=0

To see the world through the
eyes of a child again.
Oh, what a treat

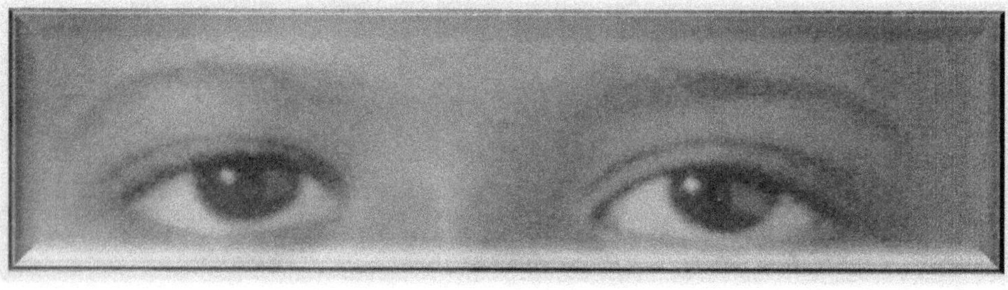

TIGHTROPE 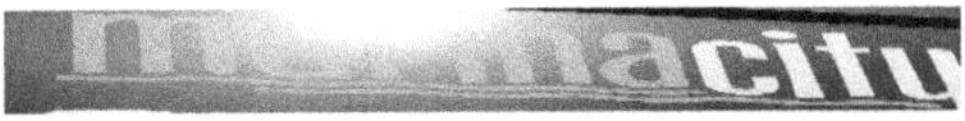 *NICK WALLENDA*

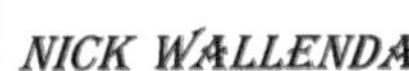

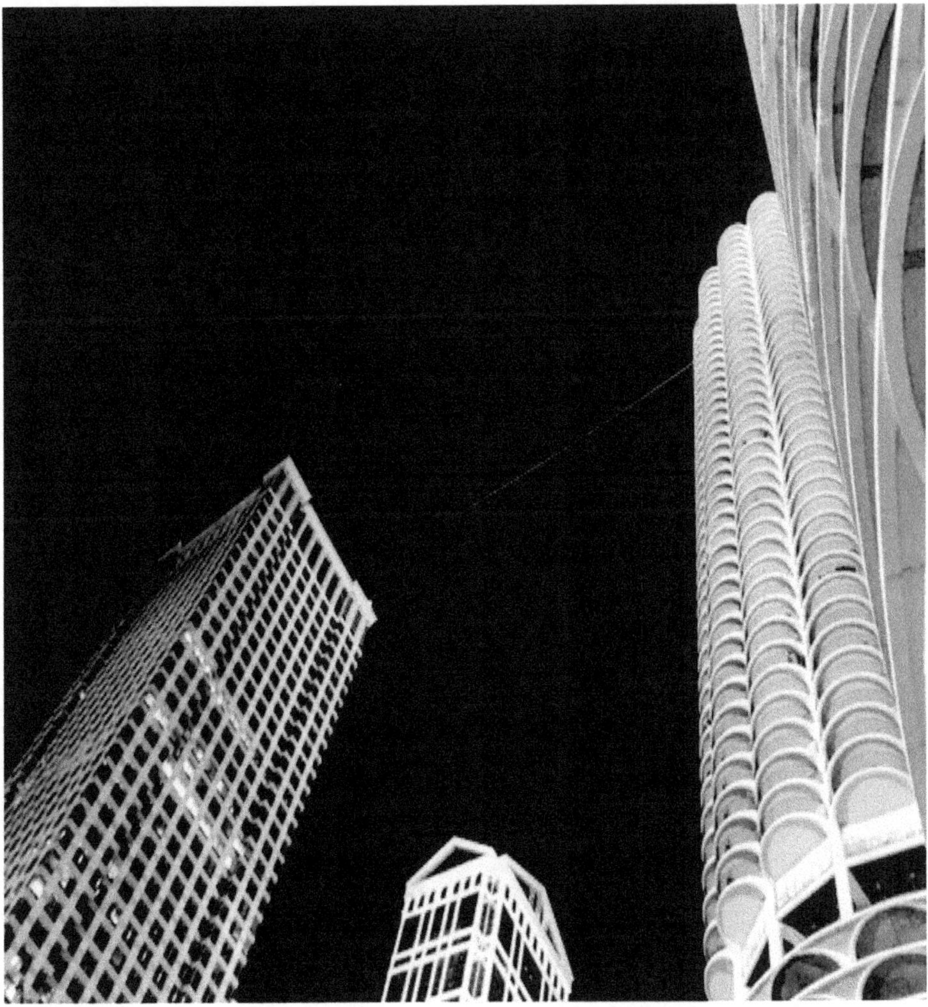

PHOTOGRAPH ASCJR

Additional copies of *Deer in the Headlights, etc.* can be ordered by sending a check or money order or purchase order if you are a school or business $10.95 + $0.95 (mailing and handling) = $11.90

Colley Enterprises
300 N. State St.
4230
Chicago, IL 60654

- **Free mailing and handling for orders of Ten (10) copies or more.**
- **Please include name and address where item is to be sent unless same on check.**
- **Book will be mailed within 7-10 days upon receipt of order.**
- **If sent as a gift, please indicate so in the ordering and a gift card will be sent for an additional $0.60**

Also, can be purchased with debit or credit card from:

PayPal by using ColleyA2@aol.com

The City of **C**hicago; The City for **E**veryman: tough, gritty, intellectual:

Actors: (Harrison Ford, Larenz Tate, Kim Novak, Karl Malden, Gary Sinise, Jesse Williams, Mitzi Gaynor, Jeremy Pivens, Joe Mantegna, Terrance Howard, Vince Vaughn, Raquel Welch, Aiden Quinn, Jenny McCarthy, Mr. T., Michael Shannon, Orson Wells, Virginia Madsen, Keke Palmer, Bill Petersen, Jeff Garlin, Justin Hartley – lived: Marlon Brando, Golda Meir, Amelia Earhart, Halle Berry, The Marx Brothers, Quincy Jones, L. Frank Baum, Mahalia Jackson, Muhammad Ali), scholars, sport teams, concert halls, I-90, pizza, pubs, The Chicago Tribune, hotels, architecture, mosques, **Filmmakers**: (Mike Nichols, Carl Seaton, Vincente Minnelli, Melvin Van Peeples, Michael Zemeckis), opera, expressways, housing, RTA, CTA, Ravinia, CTA, CPS, **Musicians**: Ramsey Lewis, Dinah Washington, Earth, Wind and Fire, Bob Fosse, Lou Rawls, Quincy Jones, Buddy Guy, Chance the Rapper, Kanye West, Donny Hathaway, Sam Cooke, Lou Rawls, Von Freeman, Common, Muddy Waters, Chaka Khan, Herbie Hancock, Mel Torme, AACM, Oscar Brown Jr., Gene Krupa, Curtis Mayfield, Justin Tranter, Albert Ammons, Michelle Williams, Minnie Riperton, Mavis Staples, Staple Singers, Henry Threadgill, Chicago, Billy Corgan, etc., theatres, events, barbecue, businesses, restaurants, museums, The Riverwalk, festivals, **Comedians**: (Melissa McCarthy, Deon Cole, Sherri Shepherd, Sean Hayes, John Belushi, Bernie Mac, Seth Meyers, Kathy Griffin, Bob Newhart, Jayne Lynch, Jack Benny, Sheryl Underwood, Robin Williams), conventions, parks, beaches, suburbs, Boystown, transportation hubs, night life, schools,, libraries, hospitals, churches, birdwatchers, synagogues, theater companies, Chinatown, bike paths, Rte. 66, movies, golf courses, universities, The Chicago Reader, diverse neighborhoods, I-80, steak houses, Lake Shore Drive, zoos, I-94, outdoor ice rinks, skateboard parks, manufacturing hubs, Ray Croc, Eliot Ness, Bobby Fischer, Cindy Crawford, Suze Orman, Richard J. Daley, Bryant Gumbel, Richard M. Daley, Rahm Emmanuel, Pat Sajak, Harold Washington, Jane Byrne, entrepreneurs, The Chicago Defender, The Chicago Tribune, The Chicago Sun-Times, **First Ladies**: [Betty Ford, Hillary Clinton, Michelle Obama], Ethel Kennedy, John Johnson (Ebony), Hugh Hefner **Athletes**: (Derrick Rose, Dwayne Wade, Isaiah Thomas, Dick Butkus, Kevin Garnett, Dorothy Hamill), home of writers, e.g., Lorraine Hansberry, Walt Disney, Gene Siskel, Ernest Hemingway, David Mamet, Shonda Rhimes, Bob Woodward, Shel Silverstein, Irv Kupcinet, Raymond Chandler, Saul Bellow, Roger Ebert(IL), Chief Justice John Paul Stevens, and **Presidents**: Barack Obama, Ronald Reagan, Abraham Lincoln (IL), Home to present and former show clubs: [Chez Paree, London House, Mr. Kelley's, The Plug Nickel, 708 Club, The Empire Room, Club Delisa, The Green Mill, The Velvet lounge, The Playboy Club, The Gaslight Club, The Baton, Biddy Mulligan's, The Happy Medium, The Sunset Café, Checkerboard Lounge, The High Chaparral, Pepper's Hideout, The Alhambra (1961), Katerina's, Andy's, Constellation, The Rhumboogie, The Grand Terrace Café, Robert's Show Lounge, Tip Top Tap, The Lyon's Den, Lounge Ax, Medusa's, The Jazz Showcase, The Empty Bottle, The Edgewater Beach Hotel, The Apartment Lounge, The Pershing, The Living Room, plus (+)

Chicago Black Gay Bars 1950s-2021

Southside
Baby O's/Club Escape, Kitty Kat, Lin's, Martin's Den, Maxine's, Parkside, The Boulevard Room, The 411, The Jeffrey Club, The Sculpture Room
Leo's Den

Downtown
The Cellar, The Rialto

Near Northside
Den One, Foster's,169, The Ritz
Stop and Drink, The Holiday, Trade and Flavor

Robbins, Illinois
Skins

SHAZZLED

I am aware; therefore, I am.

https://www.youtube.com/watch?v=rbLICxKOpHY

https://youtu.be/5gkAfqSRtpQ

PREZZOLD

(A)   TROLL Artist Thomas Dambol
and I alone call the troll "Grozzleman"

PHOTOS ASCjr

Look to the Sky

https://youtu.be/VCmQ7x6fJgM

Dr. Albert S. Colley Jr.

FREEZIing a
SNOWFLAKE

WELCOME TO THE PAGESOF: SHURPUFFED

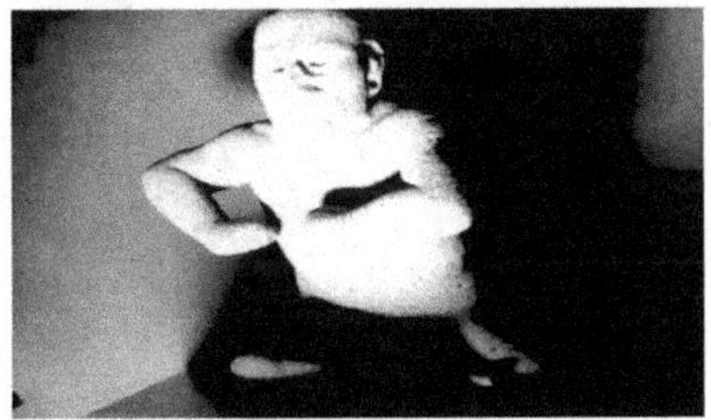

The deep breath is one of the sub-conscious pleasures of life.

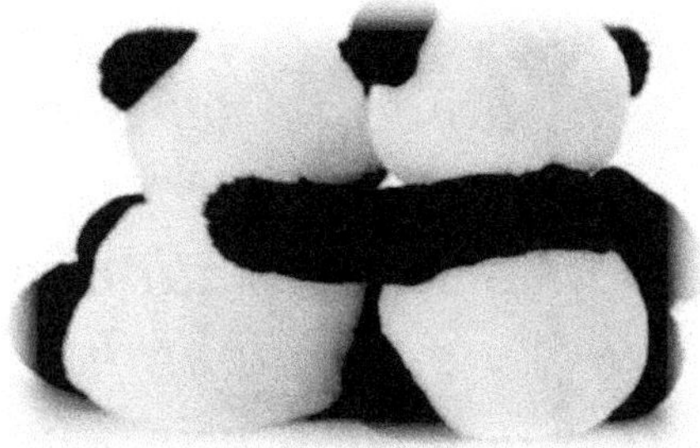

Being, living, looking Gay is not a monolith (one size fits all). 'Hey, Girl' (sic) (stereotype)

It's the accepting of each other's little differences that can make a world of difference, which gave birth to our democracy. That's what makes America Great and is the one of the major things that makes America-America. More than 'just sayin'

The only thing that the collective American psyche seems to be obsessed and care about at this point is the preservation of 'white privilege,' even if it means tolerating everything else 'going to hell in a handbag'. To see people of color or people who look different enjoy the same privileges seems to be unacceptable. It's not only in America; it is a world view as well.

So here we are 2019 back in the abyss of hatred, bigotry, and America's pursuit to "make America Great again." It seems nobody wants to confront racism, but it is Real! It exists, always has in this country, and always will as long as America' refuses to acknowledge it and take claim of it. Years and years of denial and the inability of each generation to claim its responsibility. If anything, they'll admit the claim on its ancestors. Well, this is now, and it is not your ancestors who are shooting down black boys in the streets and humiliating black women.
America can no longer afford to push this in the closet, ignore it and deny 'IT'.

This problem in my opinion is a bigger threat than North Korea, Russia, Islamic terrorism. I say this for two reasons:

1. *These are forces from without. They cannot penetrate the core.*
2. *It's more dangerous when the core is rotting and being eaten away from the inside out (for over 400yrs).*

After all the history and marches, riots, protests (peaceful and violent), blacks forgiving its oppressors, educating themselves; and blacks at times in America's history nursing (when the mother did not have milk for her own baby) because she was nurturing babies of women of Caucasian dissent. And yet Black people are still marginalized to sub-human (3/5) status.

https://www.youtube.com/watch?v=zRfcMn1TVAM

Society will never view and perceive people of color and women as an equal no matter what they do; thus, until white men step up and denounce racism and misogyny nothing will change.

Dear Deer in the Headlights,

Is prejudice today exhibited more blatantly or more subtlety?

Good morning,
You woke-up this morning. "You woke-up with two gifts: Both eyes opened." Each morning we wake-up gives us a chance to make a difference for today and tomorrow; our future, our children's future and the future of the world. YOU MATTER! Don't waste your time on things that don't matter.

Additionally, partial success of the Civil Rights movement was because the media had evolved to broadcast news instantly across the world, thus "The whole world is watching. "Now, make the whole world watch again; whatever your means of communication: text, tweet, Facebook, Instagram, phone calls, messenger. Start today, start now. 

        If you push someone off a building, they will fall to the ground unless there is some intervention to stop them from hitting the ground. Now we look at black people who as a race of people has been 'pushed off' a building. We see some black people every day who have been 'pushed off' that building where no intervention to stop them from hitting the ground took place, and we never stop to think society might be responsible for this crash these people experienced; instead, we judge and condemn them and their condition without thinking about all the years of falling - no intervention. What were they supposed to do? Defy gravity?

Pushed off the cliff:
To be born black, strike one
To be born a black male, strike two
To be born poor, strike three,
And if you're born a black gay male, oh well, you have an extra chromosome.
CRASH if no intervention
And the disadvantages continue as if you could die more than once.
They will be marginalized, criminalized, incarcerated, de-humanized as in the
good ole days; and finally looked at in guilt, disgust, judgment, and
avoidance for something of what they were but the victims.

On your way to first base:
To be born Caucasian - ball one To be born a Caucasian male - ball two
To be born into financial stability - ball three, HELLO, no strikes. You're well
on your way to first base. And the advantages continue. Unless something of
their own making occurs, they will be ok.

How many shades of blackness? Let me count the number. Oops, I forgot we already did this in slavery and post

slavery, and even gave names to the various shades, Mulatto, Mustee, Quintroon, Terceron, Quadroon,

Terceron, Octaroon, Zambo, Sacatra, Griffe, etc. Oh well.

Dear Deer in the Headlights  *,*

Let no one obstruct your vision for your brighter tomorrows.

Many Blacks are not working with dis-repair; they
are working with beyond repair. They must operate in
the despair that there are no hopes of repair.

You can lose your money and still maintain your greatness, self-respect, and your integrity; but, if you used that greatness in conjunction with compromising your self-respect and integrity to obtain that money, you are doomed. For you can always make money, lose money and get it back; but once you lose your ill- perceived greatness (because real greatness cannot be compromised), self-respect and integrity - you are doomed like a "straw in the wind," thus becoming like a bo (beau) weevil looking for a home". Look to the ruins, lost soul, that's all you're fit to inhabit.

If they had a name for cute in heaven, it would be you.

It's great to make money! But, never let that be your only…

Sass is the precursor of a troubled child.

Keep your '2-cents' unless I can it multiply by 5, and it still is relevant.

You die; I die? We die. Stars die…, and the Universe might die because these are livable, breathable entities and even these have a mortality as everything God created.

Wisdom is a gift that cannot be bought.

A better tomorrow can be yours if you only embrace that tomorrow with the same vigor as you envisioned it.

(Question) Dear Deer in the Headlights,
Should I honk? Should I *swerve*? Should I run off the road? Should I slam on the brakes? Should I keep going? Should I put my own life in jeopardy to preserve yours?

We, as mortals, cannot defy the rules of nature and the Universe. We just Can't.

"Black Lives Matter" but only in the sense in how it is beneficial to and improves white lives.

If it ain't broke, don't fix it (because your fix may break it.)

Though your flame may flicker and dim, don't let it go out.

*It's a difference from being Country and being "KUNTRY".
Just sayin'*

Deluxe is like detox. You'll never settle for regular again.

*A thought: As a 'dear,' "Are you the deer in the
Headlights?"*

*If you can't get there by land, you can always bungee
jump. Just Sayin' up for the challenge?*

After you get your ass kicked, it's time to kick ass.

All about perspective

Dear Deer in the Headlights,
Spirit never dies. It's the space where free and invisible
occupy.

Are you but a dream or a perspective yet to be understood and realized by the writer? Can I invite you to exploration that might implode and explode at the same time?

Cracked, Broken, or Shattered glass has a certain life of its own; for, it is within this state / space the fractured glass finds its own movement without the support of its whole.

Love keeps no record of wrong.

Trumpeters: Louis Armstrong, Miles Davis, Clifford Brown, Al Hirt, Herb Alpert, Maynard Ferguson, Dizzy Gillespie, Harry James, Wynton Marsalis, Chris Botti, Freddie Hubbard, and others

https://youtu.be/v-NmkQwVEqg   *https://youtu.be/hrbCWIUhggA*

No matter how high you go or how far you've gone; there will always be a force to try to pull you back down.

Sleep is analogous with Death: Death is a state of being just as sleep. When you are asleep, you are consciously unaware; but your physical body is still aware and functioning. When you have lack of physical presence (dead), your physical body is unaware, but your spirit is still aware and functioning; travelling the Universe and deciding on whether to return or become one with same.

Racism and sexism mirrors grave inadequacies in the soul, life, and heart of the racist, misogynist, and homophobe.

Trump's Base is the rue of racism.

Give me one for my service dog and one more for tonight into tomorrow.

Stay on your toes; for if they break, you still have your feet (only without branches).

Authority is based first upon reason. If you command your subjects to jump into the ocean, there will be a revolution. I am entitled to command because my orders are reasonable.

Dear Deer in the Headlights<

If black Americans are supposedly not targeted by society as many contend, then why is whenever there is a questionable policy or confrontation, especially of possible police overreaching, overreacting, and brutality only with African Americans; never with Caucasians. Can we answer this? You cannot. SAD!

'Give a man a fish and he'll eat for a day; teach a man to fish and he'll eat for a lifetime.' True that but give a man a fish today and he might understand how to fish tomorrow. You don't give him that fish today and he might perish along with his potential. In defense of underprivileged children, it's difficult to learn when you're hungry.

Discrimination in Housing comes in many shapes, shades, nuances and should shame all who perpetuate it and its regulatory and deregulatory sanctions against a minority getting ahead through housing and ownership. Just another (Make) America(n)(Great) systemic construct to keep power in the hands of a few.

ARE YOU A FRIEND ONLY TO BE SHALLOWED AND AWAKENED IN THE DEEP TOMORROW?

DON'T PRETEND TO BE WHAT YOU DON'T INTEND TO BE.

Perception precedes interpretation, which then becomes one's reality.

Dear Deer in the Headlights, 

Many Caucasians embrace and try to emulate Black culture, while at the same time loathing for the people who created that culture.

Catch yourself before you're caught.

Sometimes (our) silence drowns out the audibility of the voices of those who dare to question and challenge the status quo, leading to the captivity of the mind and spirit.

Don't let anyone take you faster than you're willing to go.

People don't die; they simply move on to a new existence.

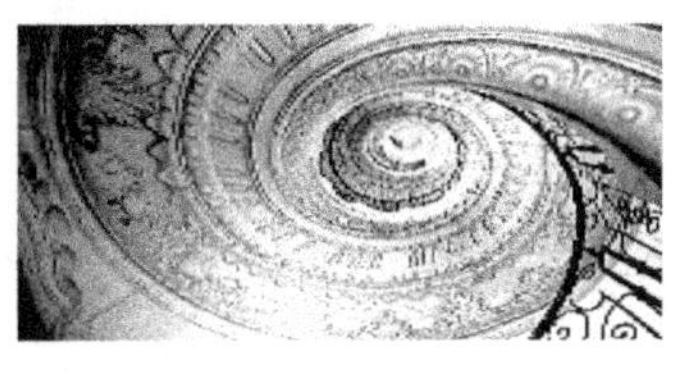 *Perception-and then - perspective.*

After I die, please do me a favor: promise to stay in touch.

You can't buy class. ...and, unlike love – you never

lose it.

Worry is 'one' thing; anticipation is another.

Worry does not take away tomorrow's troubles. It takes away today's peace.

Sometimes what we project is not indicative of what's inside or of what we feel inside.

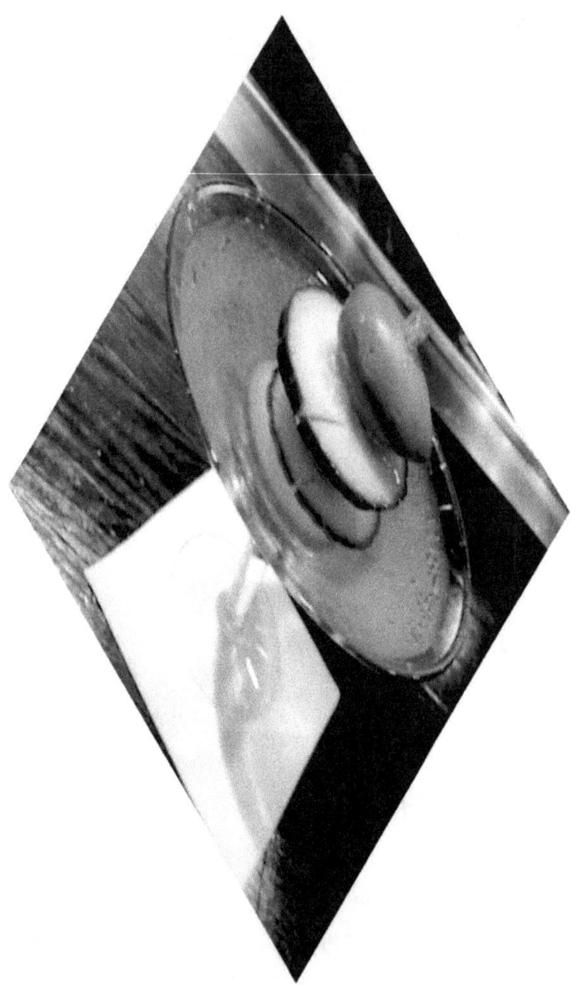

Life is so much simpler when you stop trying to explain
yourself to others and just do what works for you.

When you think about getting rich at any cost, also think about how many houses can you live in at one time?; how many rooms can you occupy at one time?; how many cars can you drive at one time?, etc...?
ASCSR/ASCjr

When you come through the vaginal connect, and win,
You're exhausted. Thus, 9-month; voila, a breath is taken
unto the 'journey of life' - and Death...

Love always comes our way if only for a day; if only for an hour. song lyric

White male dominance and supremacy which is woven into the American experience.
If a minority challenges a Caucasian male, they become a threat to their 'life,' notwithstanding only their physical life but the life of the privilege of being a white male; especially, when it comes to a challenge by a black male. Many times, when police say, "I felt my life was in imminent danger and that's why I shot," they mean psychological life as well as perhaps their physical life: It is a gross challenge to their very existence. The nerve of a black questioning them, a Caucasian male. It's an affront.

To be absent from the body is to be in the presence of the Divine.

An autistic child is a child who yearns for understanding from others to really see him(her) and their specialness.

Just as when you were a child, death was the last thing on your mind - if, on your mind at all; to many Seniors who view life as closing in on them, death is the first thing on the mind - if, not sometimes the only thing… and then it becomes an issue of 'one more time '.

Whenever you think about saying, ' I Wish";
instead, say, "I think I would love it if…"

Let your ideas go from being a caterpillar: protected – until it's ready to be a butterfly.

The P's*: Perfect, Power Poised, Produce, Prejudice, Pride, Procrastinate, Prosecution, Pulsate, Promote, Post, Picture, Punctuate, Pizza, Period, Planet, Picasso, Platform, Pig, Pedal, Process, Procedure, Point-of-View, Praying, Plain, Pressured, Paganini, Prophet, Press, Pleasant, Poetic, Precocious, Premier, Precious, Prince, Peep, Priceless, Poetry, Pi, Pure, Plato, Pretty, President, Plane, Proof, Plow, Put, Praise, Pension, Prescription, Physics, Pistol, Petal, Pinnacle, Pet, Pace, Push-Pull, Plenty, Profit, Pensive, Pound, Planet, Prestige, Pest, Part, Proposal Pinch, Priced, Pierced, Prime, Pious, Person, Profile, Peace, Paint, Pants, Politics, Prose, Point, Proper, Pose, Pass, Prior, Persecution, Playing, Place, Park, Principle, Princess, Pill, Pop, Popsicle, Police, Policy, Philanthropy, Perpetuity, Principle, Physical, Panic, Pharmacy, Pitch, Pick, Plot, Paraphrase, Paradise, Pervasive, Perish, Parade, Parody, Party, Pea, Pay, Pre's, Protest, Protect, Preserve, Palace, Permanent, Pal, Paralyze, Prize, Poker, Par, Pro, Patrol, Pacific, Plume, Patron, Pathos, Paths, Preserve, Portable, Possibilities, Puma, Program, Project, Pummel, Public, Private, Pope, Page, Plant, Prism, Prison, Piece, Paper, Papa, Purpose, Penny, Panda, Presto, Privilege, Process, Penis, Position, Positive, Plain, Posthumously, Plethora, Pasture, Pastry, Plateau, Pier, Put, Pepsi, Precious, Pryor, Private-Public, Peter-Paul, Proxy, Prosecutor, Protection, Prostitution, Pulley, Purchase, Present-Past, Ping Pong, Proof, Pout, Pour, Poop, Poor, Principal, Poe, Potato, Pistachio, Plateau, Polar, Pollster, Priest, Promise, Premier, Phase, Pharaoh, Prime, Phone, Print, Photo, Perjury, Peanut, Prejudicial, Phenomenal, Prediction, Predicate, Platonic, Prevalence, Precedence, Precision, Plummet, Puppet, Puzzle, Prosper, Portion, Potent, Portrait, Portfolio, Puberty, Paranoia, Practice, Pogonophobia, Popcorn, Prom, Pyramid, Party, Poverty, Pillar, Pale, Poll, Prevent, Peculiar, Perpetual*
(Pick a letter, any letter, and do it catch-as-catch-can over a few days)

Political clamor is but the blustering, innocuous - although sometimes - obnoxious utterances of buffoons.

The Shadows Fall I <u>and you repose</u> in the flow of the sunset

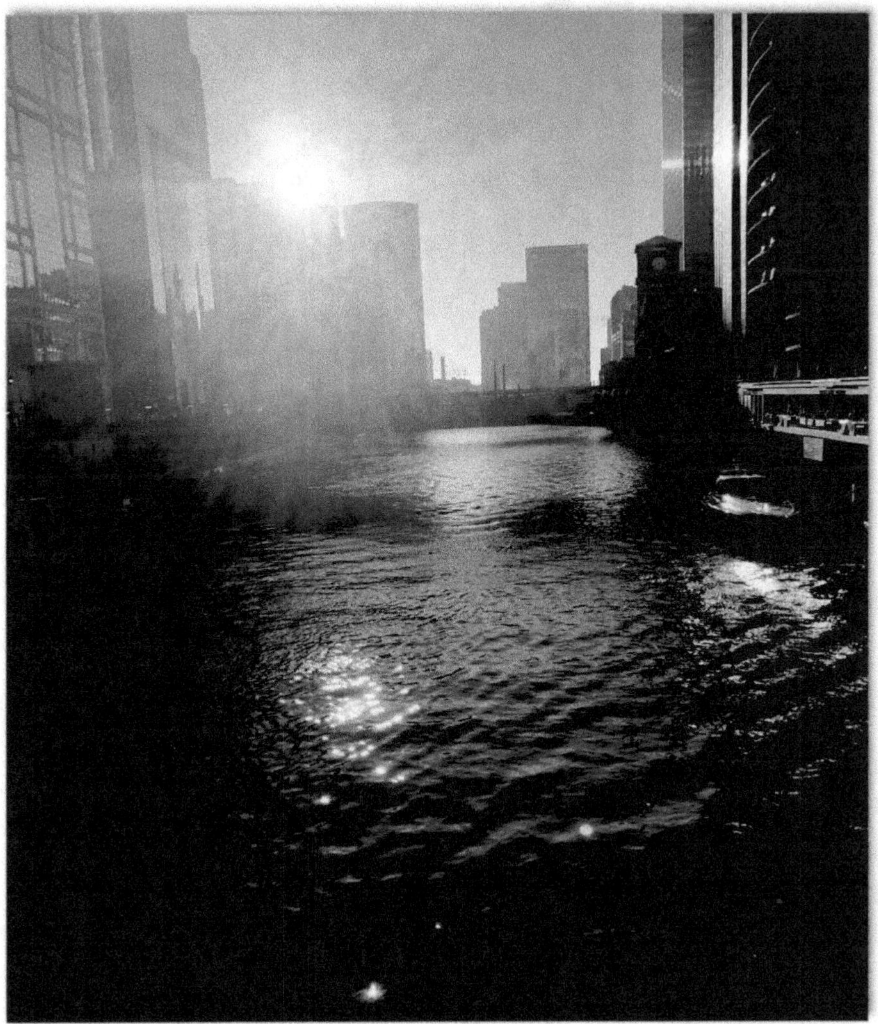

ASCjr photographer

A glass of port is the marijuana of wine.

A martini is the marijuana of alcohol.

Ok, Caucasian male/female, it's time for you to step up and assist and mentor young lost white youth who probably did not have the guidance you had and/or were able to give your offspring. Can you do that? Might make a difference.

Rotate through the fruits and vegetables; and, of course, some pasta in moderation.

WAFFLE: Left to Right, Up and down – Spin…breakfast   anyone?

Dear Deer in the Headlights,

In the broadest sense, Caucasian males objectify everything. And, view everything through the lens of 'how can it benefit me?'.

Do not cry because it's over; smile because it happened.

Each day has its own flavor.

HYPERLINK "https://itunes.apple.com/us/album/heres-to-life/638572229?i=638572352" \t
"_blank" https://itunes.apple.com/us/album/heres-to-life/638572229?i=638572352

They(re) ain't never gonna be another you.

You it!

Be who you are until you are no more.

Dear Deer in the Headlights,
Be happy; Love and be Loved.

Complacency is a major regret in and of hindsight.

The American justice system is bias toward minorities who are guilty until proven innocent instead of the other way around.

The truth is in the fruit.

How dreadful knowledge of the truth can be when there's no help in the truth.

At the age of 40 or so, go to the mountaintop as the eagle does; sharpen your beak; come back, and take flight.

Somehow life becomes quite different when it's not about you but about loving other people.

Men do not attract that which they want, but that which they are.

Left-handed racism: *the white supremacist murderer of 9-bible study black participants in a Charleston S.C. church, the police went so far in this subliminal/systemic racist move to stop to buy the killer a hamburger before taking him to the station because the white killer told the white officers he was hungry. EXPLAIN. You cannot.*

Just keep bringing the body sooner or later the mind will follow.

What is the "Soul"? It is something we cannot define; it defines itself. And everyone has a one., We often walk and subsequently wear out our (physical) sole. So, shall I bow to the whims of the world (sole) or seek eternity (Soul).

Everything should be as simple as possible, but no simpler.

All animals – but man – know life is to be enjoyed.

Sometimes in life it's ok not to be ok.

Don't let the untruth unravel your truth.

Unless you are put in a situation where you can experience a situation, can you understand the situation or possibly a similar situation?

Whatever you could have possibly experienced in this earthly realm can only pale in comparison to the after-life.

Relax and unfurl those toes. You're not the wicked witch from the west. Or are you?

Do not make runnin' for Jesus a chore. Make it a mission.

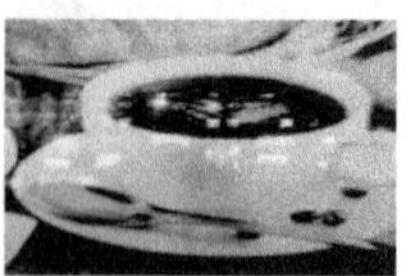

You can dream your worst nightmare into reality if you obsess over it.

Don't let your yesterday become your reality for your tomorrows.

My condensed vision for education as a school leader is to provide a nurturing environment that will encourage the maximization of students' potential to allow them to achieve theirs' and society's goals, ensuring in the short term; thereby, creating in the long term the path to make their dreams become a reality.

The whole child needs to be addressed. Therefore, learning needs to include such things as life skills, character development, sportsmanship, appreciation for multi-culturalism and diversity, what it means to be a good citizen.

Our collective stories are universal and forever; our individual personal existences are a 'maybe' and finite.

There is no limit to true vision. "I saw a man chasing the horizon. I stopped him and said," "You can't." I said, "You lie." And ran on. Educators should instill in their students to chase the horizon, and instill in them, when someone says to you, "You can't." You just continue because the future is in front of you just as the horizon.

Reminder your life is not even a moment in time compared to the existence of the world, not to mention the Universe.

Dear Deer in the Headlights,

Are you running to? Are you running from?; Are you running in place? In any event just keep running...

What will that last minute be like leading up to that last breath? 60.45.30.15.10...

Never make suicide an option as a solution.

Make life the only option.

https://youtu.be/VCmQ7x6fJgM

To be or/and to be is the only question. - No debate; discussion -

What is romance if it's not with the one you love.?

Keep the Faith, lest you lose your soul.

Being black while driving

Being black while walking down the street

Officer cleared in teen's slaying

Police board finds '12 shooting in back of head justified

Being black while cooking

Being black while at the swimming pool

Being black while at the park

Being black while having fun... Call police...Arrest

Being black while in public next?

Creative people operate on creative time and not people or perceived time.

...And then the physical dead communicate with the other physical dead through the still alive mind and spirit. While still communicating with one albeit on a conscious and/or sub-conscious state of being; and, thus the spirit has its choices and preferences as to how to communicate in this other realm of existence.

Let us not concern ourselves with preserving the supremacy of one race over others, but in preserving humanity.

Dear Deer in the Headlights,
If butterflies taste with their feet, what if we as humans had been created to taste with our nose, feel with our 👀 👀 eyes (now that's an interesting and amazing one), smell with our ears, hear through our tongue, taste with our touch? Mad, you say?

FIVE OF A KIND
https://youtu.be/PHdU5sHigYQ

(TO the LEFT, TO the LEFT
https://youtu.be/7PzxnOxzZEo

(WHO RUN THE WORLD?)
https://youtu.be/VBmMU_iwe6U

IN THE MIDDLE *http://youtu.be/jc821E-AJxl*
https://youtu.be/n7-T8FSUQ_w

GAME OVER

https://itunes.apple.com/us/album/its-all-in-the-game/528123873?i=528124011

Consciousness of a situation at the threshold of a door is the beginning of thought *and* (maybe) "lights, action, camera".

Let limitations be your imagination
Let possibilities be your infinite
Let the number of tries be your 1, 2, 3(KO/SO).

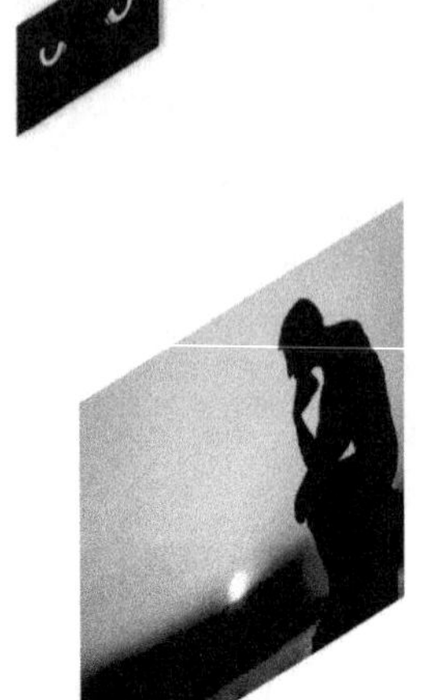

The word 'Nigger' is the one-word African Americans and only African Americans can use; however, an explanation for this is yet to be explained.

Racism is one of the founding bedrocks of America - took root in a rock (Plymouth Rock). No? You can strike it, no water only blood and weariness with no yield.

Listen to understand rather than listen for your opportunity to respond.

Racism has been institutionalized, systemized and now metastasized to the point of 'no consequences' for it; nor a stigma for one who is infected with it.

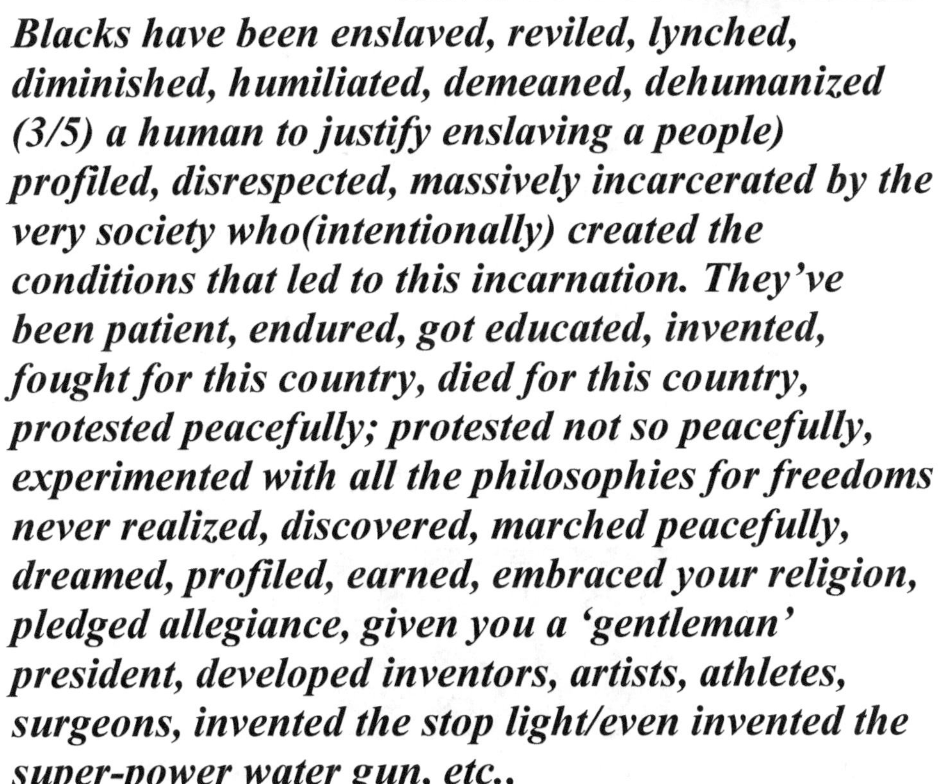

WHAT DO BLACKS, ESPECIALLY BLACK MALES, HAVE TO DO?

Blacks have been enslaved, reviled, lynched, diminished, humiliated, demeaned, dehumanized (3/5) a human to justify enslaving a people) profiled, disrespected, massively incarcerated by the very society who(intentionally) created the conditions that led to this incarnation. They've been patient, endured, got educated, invented, fought for this country, died for this country, protested peacefully; protested not so peacefully, experimented with all the philosophies for freedoms never realized, discovered, marched peacefully, dreamed, profiled, earned, embraced your religion, pledged allegiance, given you a 'gentleman' president, developed inventors, artists, athletes, surgeons, invented the stop light/even invented the super-power water gun, etc.,

Dear Deer in the Headlights,

Is social media a move forward for humanity or will it be remembered as the toxin to 'years gone by' social interactions?

YES, WE KNOW WE WERE Showered with insincere platitudes and vicissitudes. AND WHAT YOU HID were True Feelings

Dear Deer in the Headlights,
People don't die; they simply move into a new
existence.

Don't quit your Daydream.

It's all about matters of the heart.

Getting rid of someone or something to gain

someone's favor or something is a zero-sum game
with no winners. (casino talk: push)

If you can't be with the one you think you love, choose the one with
the "Wit"; and if that doesn't work, then choose the "Magic".

Awareness is the defining element of one's reality.

Is thou but a dream to be revered only after the dawn has become a ' HellO'.

Prank. Push - Pull
Precede Precedents
Photographed Physical Physiques
Punctuated Pulp Punch
Precious Phenomenal Personal Persona
Peeps, Peeped—-Ping....... Pong, POPSICLES!

Dear Deer in the Headlights:

Chicago Fire, or does this herald the plight of planet earth gone ignored in an illusionary concept of an ungraspable idiocy of we mere mortals that we are the be all and end all; the...? Will this be planet earth in 2040??

Sometimes (your) silence drowns out the audibility of those whose voices have dared to speak out, question and challenge, which can lead you to lifetime of captivity and subjugation of the mind and spirit.

I would rather be a 'lone voice in the wilderness' than a group voice.

We are not stuck in time; there is no thing as 'Time'. It is an illusionary, delusionary concept humanity decided to embrace as to try to the explain the mere passage of me.

We cannot put any race over the human race. We will learn to live together, or we will accept perishing together. However, I implore you not to choose perishing for the fleeting self- aggrandizement of an ill-perceived privilege that was born out of the aggression, repression, and suppression of minorities and the underprivileged. Note: this is a world issue.

Now the fear of the majority is that they will lose this ill-perceived privilege. And even worse, they will become the victims of their own construct.

Lies are elusive; truth is inclusive.

Sometimes you cannot always physically smile, but you can always spiritually smile.

Might (If) I have entered in that open door when it appeared in a third realm out of nowhere? I expect only those who or will have such an experience to think and understand.

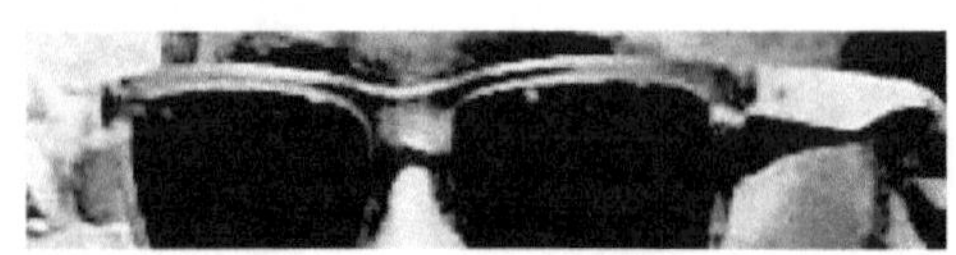

SHURPUFFED

SHURPUFFED

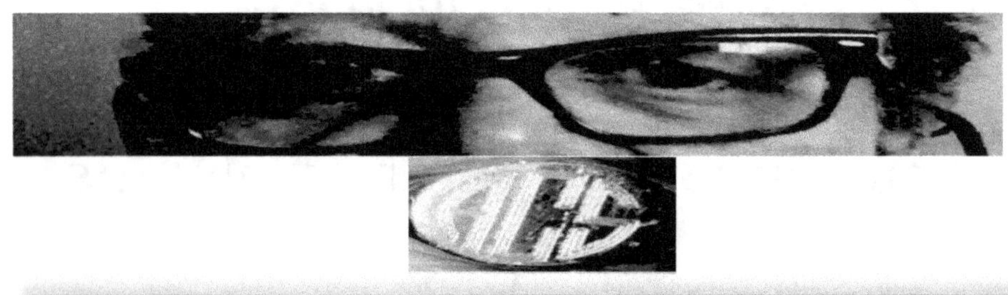

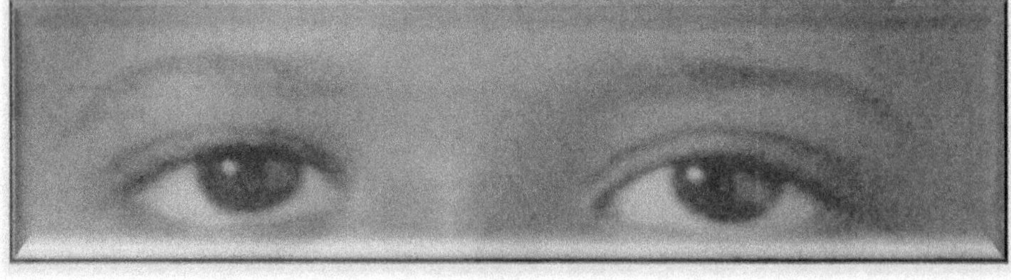

White America created the "race card." How else could it be played. Hello, Trump.

Do animals think and if they do, what do they think about? They probably think about the craziness of humans.

Racism and prejudice are more about money and greed than hatred: it keeps the oppressors with a lot more wealth.

As in slavery, slavery was not about subjugation of people for the sake of subjugation. It was about the purpose of the subjugation, cotton-picking for the sake of making the subjugators money.

Leaders and managers run to problems to ameliorate and fix, not away from problems.

Leaders take charge when there is a crisis, and not become one of the ones who need and depend upon others to lead.

2

As in La Cage aux Folle, "I am who I am." I write and post this with no ill-will and malice towards none, I offer a reflection for persons of thoughts. Having said that,

Why are marginalized Black men so angry and some not so unmarginalized black men angry as well? Where does one think that anger comes from? It goes way past when they were even born. They want to be Seen. They want to be Heard. They want to be Recognized - even if it's negative recognition albeit being loud, wearing pants off butt, being more aggressive in a situation than the situation warrants, They're trying to say **I'm here** as opposed to neither here nor there.

I'm just not an invisible man. I'm a man who was stolen and taken from my Homeland and have ~yet~ to realize a new home. --To be looked upon systematically by white America with disdain and displeasure as if somehow the conditions they find themselves is all their fault; And should somehow be viewed through a different lens than their white counterpart.; And then to be incarcerated in record numbers by a racist justice system; And even after be released from prison be denied the right to acquire gainful employment, thus driving them right back into marginalization and crippling and keeping them and their families marginalized, economically, educationally, emotionally, spiritually, and most importantly, a husband and father of whom the family cannot depend; making many black families by design dysfunctional, leaving them unable to acquire what their white counterparts have. Example: White family income is 1 0x's that of a Black family, ~TEN times. And most importantly a race of people who have been lied to time and time again with the "if you only..." only to be miffed by unrealized promises and dreams promises and dreams that are only reserved to this day for the oppressor, not the oppressed.

3

In General, Black people have no release valve. Blacks our trapped in Camus' *No Exit*, Langton's *A Dream Deferred*, Cleaver's *Soul on Ice*, Ellison's *The Invisible Man*, M. J.'s *They Don't Really Care About Us*, and Dorsey's *Precious Lord Take my Hand* cause I just can't take this ~ hell ~ anymore. Blacks are just a boiling cauldron about to or for some, already at the boiling point: tried servility (slavery) ~ did not work; tried civility towards suppressor ~ did not work; fought valiantly in Civil War, WWI, WWII (of note,

Black soldiers were asked at Christmastime to sit outside in the cold while white American troops sat inside, partying with German troops. Yes, it's true (know your history); financial independence (Black Wall Street whites destroyed) ~ did not work; Korean War, Viet Nam War, Afghanistan War ~ did not towards oppressor ~ did not work; tried assimilation ~ did not work; tried benevolence ~ did not work; tried the legal system ~ did not work; tried EDUCATION ~ did not work; and a black president ~ did not work! (and finally tried for whites only to a non-conventional President that is attempting to take blacks only take blacks back more than a half a century ~ has not worked for anyone but white Americans.

People say, 'Oh race, Who wants to talk about that?' I Do.! White Americans don't want to talk about racism. And many try to deny its very existence. ~could it be because racism has always and even today benefited white Americans and their children from slavery to Jim Crow to today? ~<u>REALITY</u> Do you have another explanation? What all America needs to realize if we don't address this issue once and for all, the very existence of this country, including white America is in peril. Because blacks are so embedded in America and intertwined with white Americans that whatever affects blacks impacts white America too.

 As I posited in the 70s, akin to systemic racism fueled by centuries of marginalization, design, degradation, and disenfranchisement of minorities, those in the majority will never accept a minority as an equal in this country - no matter what the minority does, never have; never will because they perceive the recognition of the minority as being an equal to be counterproductive to their interests as opposed to seeing it as a way for all to move forward - interconnected for the making of a better country and world.

WHILE SITTING IN A PILE OF BANANAS, IT SQUISHED; I RELEASED A NEEDED HOLLER

Was from 1965 to 2015 but a vacation for blacks and other minorities - 50-years? Hey minorities, vacation is over. Reality, ~ you have gone from involuntary slavery to wake-up voluntary slavery.

It was partly because of the cowardice of many that a few are able to seize governments.

5

White men have   the right to bear arms;
minorities have the burden of being the targets of that right.

What matter what day it is when it is no longer a concern for you?

How can society blame the condition black fathers find themselves when that same society created the framework for this outcome? (Think about it.)

The more as an African American man and an educated one I tried to say 'it's not about race' the more I arrived at the realization that It is.

To keep one race dominating another race is about money and greed. Example: White Household incomes are 10x's that of African Americans.

*As we reflect on the end of the yin-yang
decade. Let us think of how far we've moved forward; and how far
we've journeyed backwards. I guess all things in time,* 🫠
To Expand:

1. *Forty acres and a mule, never realized*
2. *Educationally equality, never realized on any level*
3. *Generational pass down of wealth, never realized*
4. *Awarded the respect of being recognized and legitimatized
   as a people: Different in tone, in perspective, Different in
   'sup' and 'hi', and bye and 'later', but Equal, never realized*

*Rate the 5-senses as you personally see them ranking in
importance on scale of 1-5 with 5 being the most
important and 1 being the least rate the five senses:*
Hearing -
Seeing -
Smelling -
Touching -
Tasting -
(Intuiting) -

*This is not America and not who we are. Yes, it is:
American Indian, Slavery and chains. Jim Crow*

*Babies be having their own conversation: Bluh blu bluh blu
bla bla Bligh Bluh*

What we are failing to realize White and Black America is that when we hurt one of us, we hurt all of us near term and long-term. Example: The trauma of white assault on the black community in the Chicago White assault 1919 on the black community left a lasting legacy we're still dealing with today to the detriment of our communities, stress on our law enforcers, suspicion, and distrust and why? Hatred! the black street gang. "To be sure, the 1919 riot (Chicago) contributed directly to Black gang formation in Chicago, as Black males united to confront hostile White gangs who were terrorizing the Black community.
James C. Howell, "The History of Street Gangs in the United the United States.
(We cannot continue to blame the perpetrated upon as the perpetrators. At some point the perpetrators need to own up to their iniquities, however painful.)

<u>HEY GUYS - Blacks, women, gays, transgender, older, younger, SINGLES (when you gonna get married?) (when you gonna have kids? What, you got a problem down th...?Are you Gay? Are you mixed?</u>

Maybe those who are shouting, 'They should go back!' if they don't like the America of Trump should go back if they don't like the Constitution.

Some "Born again Christians" say, ' I don't do the things I used to do: 'smoke, drink, and step on people's feet'. Well, some born again Christians still smoke, drink, and sometimes have the need to step on people's feet and perhaps they are on a spiritual journey and quest that does not include judgement of who other people are. You see being a Christion is not about the aforementioned. Are they welcome in your church? Are they asunder? Hmm?

If one partakes of drink and/or drugs, does that make them any less in the eyes of the Creator? Does that make you anymore because you espouse none of this, but sit in judgment of others? Yeah, one may do all of this, but you have no idea of their bond and relationship with God.

My favorite pastime is 'THINKING'. 

IF YOU'RE A MINORITY, THE SYSTEM KEEPS ITS FOOT ON YOUR NECK; HOLDING YOU AND THE ONE FOOTED FROM GOING FORWARD.

Every baby is considered cute until proven otherwise, thus comes the phrase "innocent until proven guilty" You think?

Why are marginalized Black men, especially young black men so angry. and some unmarginalized black men angry as well. Where do you think that anger comes from? It goes way past when they were even born. They want to be seen. They want to be Heard. They want to be recognized even if it's negative recognition, even

*if it's negative recognition albeit being raucous, wearing pants off butt, being more aggressive in a situation than the situation warrants, etc. Perhaps they are trying to say **I'm here** as opposed to neither being here nor there.*

White America created the "race card." How else could it be played. Hello, Trump.

"Special" has no definition. It speaks for itself:

Ted Williams Serena Williams Joe Louis Stephen Curry Usain Bolt Jim Thorpe

Michael Phelps Pele Babe Ruth W. Chamberlain Barbra Streisand Ali Roberto Clemente

There is no greater pleasure in Life than to be 'pain free,' physically and mentally.

Best way to predict the future is to invent it. .Langston Hughes called-it a "Dream Deferred" now it is a dream never to be realize.

Nothing thinks like hurt.

America would rather see guns in the hands of the mentally ill white person rather than in the hands of a black man.

If you cannot sleep, you cannot dream. And if you cannot dream, you will soon grow weary

The more as an African American man and an educated one tried to say 'it's not about race' the more I arrived at the realization that that's It.

Haunches are like hunches both to be cognizant (of).

The very essence of who we are in a quest of faith and believing in a Higher Power can be anchored in a child's definition of faith, 'Kiss it up to God'.

We know that God keeps His promises; whereas, in our frailty, we do not.

When a person of tremendous talent dies, does that talent die as well or does it become a part of universal ethos?

To relatives of senior citizens - Upon a senior's demise, it's more about what's inside the cabinet than the looks on the outside; especially if the senior could cook.

In a flood, 'Run!'

Does it matter if it's a real ghost(threat) or (just) one in your mind, 'Run!'

'Blame' is not the answer.

How the culture has changed:
Oaths mean nothing
Truth means nothing
Facts mean Nothing
Legislators doing the will of the people means nothing
Office of the President means nothing,
only the person in it matters
The Intelligence Department means nothing
Your will means nothing
Foreign interferences mean nothing, etc., etc., ...
And still we sit.

Empathy in any art form is the 'Key' now once you're in the door, what else you got?

<u>Explicit</u>

Here is a lesson to learn: When You screw a brother. you've screwed all brothers who encounters that screwed brother, but especially you: sell-out slave mentality!

⊙ DING – You sank to the bottom. THOUGHT YOU WERE SMARTER. NOTHING PERSONAL. EPOX ON YOU... SHIT HAPPENS: Be especially careful of what you eat and don't upset anyone who cooks for you.

Strange things can happen once "stuff" gets in your stomach. Try as best you can under the circumstances to sleep. Proud of yourself, big man?

 DING

Life is like a musical chord: Harmony is the usual and pleasant to the ear and then comes that necessary dissonance to refresh.

Bubbles are always fun until they burst.

<u>Two thoughts on the 'Soul'</u>

1) The Soul is the manifestation, connection and completion of all mankind with nature in direct contact with the Creator.
2) The Soul is The "Spirit" and all the spirits who pass and have passed through you now and in the past.

It is strange as if the moment that just happened, Didn't.

Systemic Racism, the 400-yr pandemic continues to kill Black people physically, mentally, financially, emotionally, spiritually; our children, our parents, our friends, our brothers, Sour sisters while pretending otherwise. It is no longer depriving blacks of their rights; it is starving blacks of their rights, well, if they ever had any to begin; *Depriving and starving them of the rights all others enjoy now, in the past, and in the future!*

Reform of Law Enforcement is good in theory but until you can reform an officer's heart, change him perspective, and assist him in gaining a sense of respect and compassion for those who are of a different color and/or background and may have had different experiences from him/herself; it's all for naught.

Additional training and licensing for law enforcement is great, but the heart cannot be trained and licensed and neither can compassion for your fellow person.

Emmett Till Age14   George Floyd   L. McDonald Age 17 Tamir Rice Age 12 Antwan Rose Age 13

Trayvon Martin(17 yrs. old) Lynching   Michael Brown Age 18)   Philando Castille   Sandra Bland

Freddie Gray Jr   Eric Garner   Jacob Blake Marcellus Stinette(19))   Brianna Taylor

86 Black Men and Boys killed by law enforcement as of 09/2020
newsone.com/playlist/black-men-boy-who-were-killed-by-police/

WHERE CAN A BLACK MAN GO FOR HELP?? POLICE, COURTS, PAROLE BOARDS, JOBS, MENTAL HEALTH

For Real:

The question. "Who this nigga think he is?" did not originate with Black people, but White people when a
Black man was tryin' to get ahead, especially in business and finance. Case in point, the same as the word, nigger as we bastardized to "nigga" did not originate from Black people but whit people. The discrimination of Black people in black communties based on the hue did not originate with Black people but White peoples. (Are you lighter than a paper bag. And the king of it all that Black people are still buying into, while at the same time trying to refute, "If you have
a drop black blood, you are Black."
Black people argue, 'Oh, my grandad was white; I'm bi-racial because my dad is white." "I'm better than you because I'm a lighter skin." Tell it to the next policeman who stops you or the next judge you face.'
Yeah 'Face' black face. That's the point. Get It!

Same as with "crabs in the barrel", when one begins to climb, and we pull them down. This was not originally a Black construct but emerged out of what whites would do to hold Blacks down. Somewhere this construct was translated to Black people problem with each other when the poison or dye cast, if you will, began when this perpetration was set in motion by design.
All this with the mindset of whites who put forth these constructs as Blacks not being intelligent enough to see through the charades.

FACILITIES, EMPATHY, COMPASSION UNEQUAL ED SYSTEM, HISTORY, AND LASTLY AMERICA? NOWHERE!

The beginning of life is

the antithesis of.

The consolation of Life to those who have children is that when you die you have a great chance there will be at least one child to carry-on vs. childless individuals, especially those without siblings who don't have off-springs.

The two questions I would ask God if I had a chance:

1. What did you do before there was nothing?
2. May I touch you?

Is the killing of Black people an 'everyday' "oh well" and "okism" non-news event as pre-1960s?

If an animal is not prone to eat (feast on) you then why are you afraid of it? Just sayin'

BLACK MOTHERS WANT TO SLEEP AT NIGHT TOO.
BLACK CHILDREN WANT TO PLAY TOO.
BLACK MEN WANT TO FELLOWSHIP TOO!
ALL WITHOUT FEAR AS YOU DO

If I cannot ever know me then then I'll be you.

If you live without reflection, you should start questioning if you even exist.

You can't wear a crown with your head down.

Because Trump goes away, does not mean this vitriol goes away.

Blacks are not working with dis-repair; they are working with beyond repair - however, they must operate with the disrepair with no hopes of repair.

When it's a black man, you always view him through the worst lens; when it's a white man, you always view him through unfiltered lens or no lens at all.

Over 196 justices appointed during the Trump administration to do his bidding

When Society subjects one race of children from birth with hostilities and deprivation and another race the race treated unfairly exhibits frustrations and anger. Society can't blame them. Society, Step-up and claim the fact!

People discuss minorities getting in on the legalization - duh - just make it ok for the street dealer to continue to sell; thus, the little minority guy can continue to generate some revenue.
Problem solved.
Caveat: find a reasonable way to license street dealers. Supply might then meet the demand.

Trump purported to help minorities while setting all things in motion for the diminution of same.

A Black man's question to a society that oppresses him: What is there ok to do?

Settlers did to Native Americans

- Took away their economy
- Made them dependent
- Separated them
- For every action, there is a reaction example: Obama to Trump

•

Why is it so hard to admit a black man is equal or that, you are not equal to a black man? You would rather destroy the entire human race than to admit either.

You Can't Be Dead

Wake up, wake up, wake up!
You can't be dead.
Wake up, America.
BREATHE...
Come on. You're America;
you can do it!
Breathe...
I cannot breathe.
I have the knee of racism on my other's neck:
400yrs...
Now, I Can't breathe.
I'm America,
And I CAN'T BREATHE...Sigh
...Wait, wait, I got a pulse.
Finally, one America
"with liberty and justice for all."
I'm Black. I can't breathe.
Yes, you can and you will.
You are America, (too): built America.
This is not a house;
This is a HOME.

Jes-se(e) Sir Jacksoon

Could have been any son
But was born Jackson
Jes-Se(e) what he's done
Jesse(e) Jackson)

Hailed from the Carolinas, he did
Scoped the minds of the Heads
Blew off some lids
He and wife raised five kids.

People cried,
Carried the "breadbasket" for the poor.
People cried, "He's our man, for sure!"
He' s the revolver that couldn't be silenced.
Fought hard for economics and alliance.

He lifted us up
He filled our cup
Bought us 7-up
Negotiated with Burger King
Without saying "chitterling."

Got us Action That's Jes-se(e) Jackson
On the front line
Doing fine.

Jes-se(e) Sir Jackson (cont.)

Gave us Push-Excel
Christmas at the County Jail
Used his contact
Ended the firemen's contract.

Said, "Trade, not aid."
Yeah,
It's our time
to get said.

He sought The Democratic Party Nomination
Thought about a woman and he in combination
A bid for the United States Presidency
Would have ensured a January 1985 White House
residency.

Kept hope ALIVE!

Right on
Jackson
Right won Jackson.
I mean—Sir Jesse Jack-son

Because Trump goes away, does not mean
this vitriol goes away.

The new face of 'racism' post George Floyd: Suppressive, Subversive, Subliminal, Self-serving, Sanctioned, Severe, Surfaced, Spiteful, Subtle, Sub-conscious, of course Systemic; and the most derisive, Smiling or as Trump always posits, - Oh I didn't know/realize. Wink, wink

Until we see a black person's humanity, you cannot see their individuality.

Will the killing of George Floyd by a white police officer turn out to be the vaccine Racists need to make America immune (numb) to less egregious confrontations as the routes of assassinations and school shootings did?

The Society creates a situation(s)and then blame those for whom it affects; blame them for the condition(s) they find themselves.

Only through individual change in thought and of heart; and, of commitment to that change
can collective change occur and become a reality.

Black people are operating with despair and 'beyond repair, but continue to operate in spite of...'

In the long run, a deep breath is well-worth a dollar in the pocket (bank).

Racism: Do we have the strength and tenacity of universal purpose to unravel and give our youth and future generations a new world?

Be who you are until you are no more.

Do not let the untruth unravel your truth.

It is incumbent on us all, which, I believe, represents the majority of Americans to shut hatred, discord, and discrimination down of those who claim and believe it is our best interest to have America back track on social justice and equality for all - all in the name of them being so superficially at best that they and their like are America. Don't extinguish the protesters for much deserved justice. Let us extinguish those who are against justice and equality for all! We must do this and do it now. Our democracy and very existence depend on it. HATE MONGERS, DAMN YOU. WE WILL NOT FOLLOW YOUR IDIOCY. This vitriol must go away.
Justice and equality for all! We must do this and do it now.

If we do not interact with those who make us
uncomfortable,
we will never grow or have an intelligent conversation with
only half the facts or no facts at all.

One must cherish objective evaluation of persons and thoughts;
for without individuality of thought, we have nothing to base
an opinion.
Society, Step-up and claim the fact!

Ok, America

No more hiding behind the sheet of "I don't understand"
even in a fraction of a way when inequities and inequality a
race of people have endured for centuries and still now:
knee on the neck not a new phenomenon. The state of our
society then and now is not at all about blacks, but about a
white problem that for some reason they have not and
cannot seem to solve within their own race.; for blacks have
done everything possible and imaginable to redirect white
systemic racism to no avail. There is nothing more black
people can do. 56-years of the hosing of black people, dogs
biting black people, black people spat on, etc. The greatest
cynicism is the hate by white people for Black people
when they see through their schemes, winks, and for lack
of another word 'bullshit".

PART II

Dear Deer in the Headlights

There are bridges to take Caucasians back to where they originated. There are no bridges to take Blacks where they came originated.

Social opinions and media justify the ignoring of one's talents.

A (guilty) white man will more times than not be treated better when being arrested than an (innocent) Black man.

Society created the conditions by which black on black crime exists in black communities, fatherless homes through incarcerations, and lack of jobs, etc.

**FUTURE HEADLINE
(2025)
Mob storms the Capitol upon the urging of a lame duck President: 62 killed House members and 28 Senators, 34 relatives to former Congressman. Why? (Hypothetically, because) in 2021 the Senate Republicans faced to "Do the**

MAGA sent this country in the most negative direction and in the most dangerous course of the once greatest country (USA) in the World.

A message to America's lawmakers:
 Scared of losing your job? Scared of Donald Trump? Scared of losing your home? Scared of your neighbors and people not liking you? Well, you'll have plenty of time to be scared when the 'shit hits the fan.' So come out of your hole now and "STAND UP!"
There is No
defense for Black enslavement, Jim Crow, destruction of "Black Wall Street, lynching of Blacks through t he non-enforcement of 'serve and protect' turned into "serve the interests of white America and protect the notion of white privilege." Scam of "Liberty and Justice for all.

If Blacks are seen moving too fast in achieving equity, socially - and especially financially, society always seems to find a way to thwart that effort. Ex. Jim Crow, Tulsa Massacre, the dismantling of the Black family through Black male incarceration and making it more financially beneficial for a Black father to be to not be in the home than in the home.

What is "the Death?" Not what is death?

Every life path has a reward albeit different - but no less than any other. The reward is what it means to the individual who decided to take a specific path.

Humans are made on earth; angels are made in heaven.

The irretrievable sadness of reality is seeing and knowing it and then say and think otherwise.

Shall I live for present or in the future knowing, neither one changed or will ever change?

KNOWLEDGE IS KEY. THAT'S WHY one explanation might be in The Garden of Eden EVE WAS FORBIDDEN EAT of the Tree of Knowledge; PROPHETS in all cultures were TEACHERS.

A fool thinks he knows everything but knows nothing of most things.

A wise man knows he knows little about most things but knows what he knows.

I did not anticipate the simple answers would surface devoid of nuances of other perspectives and perceptions. So be it for shallowness as it is much more comfortable than to think about another opinion other than your narrow alley.

The reckless wound of reality is imaging that the reality doesn't exist.

Existence transcends non-existence.

Be like children as an adult, if you want to know something of/or about an individual, JUST ASK them...more to gain than lose, allowing you both to stay or to move forward.

Fifth graders are at the top of the food chain from baby to creating a foundation for going forward into adolescence to either look backward or forward; only to become the refuge for...

"THE CREATOR GAVE THE WORLD ENOUGH FOR EVERYONE; NO NEED TO EVER FEEL THREATENED OF LOSING (IT). YOU'RE COVERED!"

Humans die with so much knowledge and wisdom never shared.

I didn't know I was this until somebody said I was; I didn't know I wasn't this until somebody told me I wasn't.

Only when the American system that nurtures the idea of whites to be superior to non-whites will systemic perpetuation begin to erode.

A man needs a home, a space be it room, area, garage, basement, attic, patio, garden deck, closet, etc.: a space all his own both and/or physically and psychologically.

At a certain stage of existence, life you begin to fully understand life is not about ego or self-aggrandizement, but about what you brought to the world and what you leave behind; however large or small. MAKE DIFFERENCE. Do not hide your talents and gifts under the bed. Those talents were given to you to share. And if individuals feel you share those gifts and talents for personal adulation, so be it.
If you can think , you are.

To God you are; to God you'll return.

To vegetate is not fine. You were not born to vegetate. You were born to blossom. You owe it to the Creator to do so.

The media will always report the worst of a situation - if - for no other reason than to get you to pay attention.

We need to be trying more to live in harmony and understanding with all other species on the planet. That will be difficult, considering we can't live even in harmony and understanding with each other.

A little cocktail talk

A little first-hand, personal experience: After 3-drinks, wine or spirits; depending on your drink of preference - the euphoria (high) or any additional high is not enhanced with additional drinks, but only leads to diminishing of one's judgement, to physically be determined by medical doctors. Additionally, there isn't any reason to continue drinking alcohol after 3-drinks, but for something to do.

"Vita Small*" is:

A drink at the end of the night or while niceties are being exchanged to end the evening; and/or in a public place you visit after the last call; or with a friend who knows you and what this means as you state/ask the bartender or host to pour you a 1/4 to 1/3 of a drink. Ok, just a vita small (2/3) or a vita small junior (1/4). *inspired by a childhood friend*

List of possible LIFE'S TOP 10 Things to give THANKS

1. *Love of God*
2. *Life*
3. *Health*
4. *Food and Shelter*
5. *Ability to feel love and empathy for my fellow person*
6. *Blessings*
7. *Talents*
8. *Six Senses*
9. *Positioning in life to be where one is supposed to be, at the time one was supposed to be, and with whom one was supposed to be, which includes friends and relatives.*
10) *Tomorrow - for without tomorrow, we are not*

If I cannot ever know me then I'll never know you.

If you live without reflection, you should start questioning if you even exist.

You can't wear a crown with your head down.

Black was beautiful

 even before beauty was defined.

It becomes more difficult for Black people to think outside of the Box when they are physically trapped inside the very Box society is asking them to step outside of.

Why does society oppress and suppress those that enables/d them to enjoy what they have? Why? What is this pathology?

How can America ignore and not acknowledge the very thing (Black Americans) that allows them to live the life- style and benefit from the benefits that they enjoy! HELP ME UNDERSTAND.

Can YOU define who 'all' refers to in "Liberty and Justice for all?" Maybe 'all' is 100% of a human and not 3/5 of one.

Let's stop and put things in perspective: All these unjustified brutality attacks on Black people by police persons are performed by sick officers and do not (necessarily reflect) the feelings of the society at large.

"This is not who we are."...even though facts herald differently.

Malice and hate are hard to contain, not to mention control. It is the responsibility of the one infected with this insidious disease to find a cure and not for the one whose hate and malice is perpetuated to cure the problem. You thought you'd solve the problem at the time of after arriving here with Nothing; deciding to corroborate with slave traders on the Continent of Africa to export human capital as a thing to be disposed after their intended purpose of serving and making your life easier. There was no thought of the African Americans having any sense of humanness, but in able for you to justify and assuage guilt in your mind, you delegated them as three-fifths of a human. How else could your guilt be quelled, allowing you to sleep at night for over 300 years. Now you think you're going to play the same game.
I DON'T THINK SO.

<u>Interestingly</u>, the average Caucasian has at least 2% Neanderthal in their DNA vs. Blacks. Maybe this gave rise to a system of whites proclaiming if a person had 2% of black blood, they would be labeled Black. Should we then have surmised that the average white person is a Neanderthal? It appears perhaps somewhere in history whites switch the switch.

More on Race:

Whites initiated and institutionalized slavery, Jim Crow, Tuskegee, red-lining, etc., Many whites espouse, 'Oh, let it go. That happened in the past. Yes, it happened in the past and is continuing to happen now, - and - it will continue to happen in the future: 1619, 1819, 1919, 2019...2119...

(Will it ever end?)To white people who say, "Let it go." Maybe Black people could let it go if they (Black people) didn't continue to experience racism every day; And - if America

1) **recognizes and admits racism exist.**
2) **recognizes and admits racism is a systemic problem in these United States of America**
3) **Whites can let go of racism and all that springs from it going forth.**

Black kids, especially teenagers can't be a kid at the risk of being misperceived:
- Black kids can't act crazy and whacky.
- Black kids can't gather in crowds (beyond two).
- Three or more Black kids assembled
- together signals trouble to the power system.
- Black kids can't make mistakes in public because they know a mistake could bring harm to them.
- Black kids (people) cannot make any type
- of move that might be perceived as aggressive.
- Black kids (people) cannot ask questions
- nor show any type of behavior that might
- be perceived as disrespect to a policeperson.
- Black kids outdoors having fun are
- perceived as a threat that demands surveillance and a watchful eye by patrol persons.

Black kids, especially teenagers can't be a kid at the risk of being misperceived (cont.):
  ○ Black kids with perceived non-acceptable hair styles, such as dreadlocks or crowns is non-acceptable to the white community and is considered a threat that demands surveillance and a watchful eye from white patrol persons; whereas white kids with pink, purple, spiked hair, etc. is ok.

  ○ White kids can wear hoodies without impunity, AND even with their hands in the inserts. Black kids and hoodies? Well,
  ○ Black kids with hoodies demand
  ○ surveillance and have been beaten and killed for such.
    White kids (people) can live a carefree life; black kids (people) cannot.

In the author's view, Systemic Racism will not end in America because it is too advantageous financially, psychologically, emotionally, etc. to the Caucasian race and its beneficiaries; from slavery to present day. (It's a comfort for the system to continue to afford and abet Caucasians to feel superior to another individual because this feeling is inherent and has been embedded in their culture for centuries.)

49

DADS
A root (route); starter of the race.
A skipper, a hand,
a sander of men.

MOTHERS
They are the 'Y's'
The Protectors,
An attentive ear, a watchful eye;
the right touch.
They have the taste and smell
of what is best for theirs; and,
that extra sense to tie it
into a neat
package.

God is anything that anybody and everybody thinks He is, could and would be.

Sir Creator,
I could thank you for Many things, but I would just like to thank you for this One thing before I forget, and that is for "Being my Creator," and to more than mention, creating me in your (I)(m)age and likeness.

Excuse me, excuse me - God is Nothing: the absence of anything, the ultimate void, never to be grasped physically, emotionally, mentally, nor even spiritually because of limitations of our humanness ~~ But can connect with is on all these levels because of the transcendency of its nothingness.

IN CONCLUSION

Perception vs.

Perspective vs.

Perspective vs.

Perception vs.

Perception vs. Decisions

vs. Outcomes vs.

A new Perspective vs,

a change in Perspective

And – Ideally the triangle and square

Somehow becomes a

Oval Reality

When it's all said and done,
the 'World' keeps spinning

Let US pray 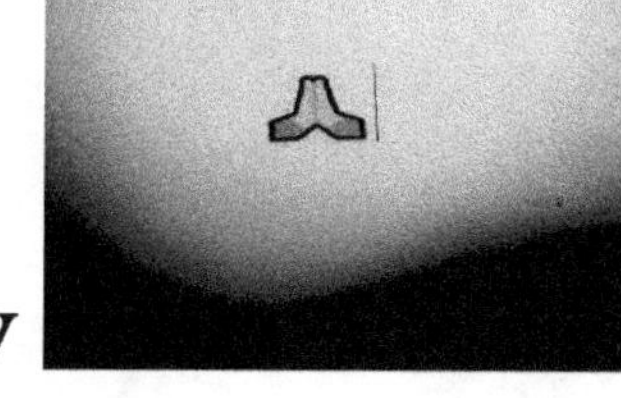 to keep it that
way. Amen

THE END